Praise for *Life: T*

"Navigating the predictable dilemmas of aging parents requires compassion, communication and a plan. *Life: The Next Phase* offers all three in a clear, concise and practical format. It is a welcomed resource for caregivers and professionals alike."

—David Solie, MS, PA, Author of *How To Say It To Seniors: Closing the Communication Gap with Our Elders*

"The underlying philosophy of stepping in (together with), not stepping over your aging parents' desires underlies this practical book's roadmap through the important areas of concern for your loved ones' present and future wellbeing."

—Grace Lebow, MSW, Co-Author of *Coping With Your Difficult Older Parent: A Guide for Stressed-Out Children*

"With clarity of purpose and well-conceived organization, this pragmatic guide provides assurance and relevant information to stressed family caregivers."

—Barry J. Jacobs, Psy.D. Author of *The Emotional Survival Guide for Caregivers: Looking After Yourself and Your Family While Helping an Aging Parent*

"Organized by the type of care needed, this book explains relevant financial and legal issues, as well as sometimes more difficult topics such as how to talk with the person being cared for about his or her needs and how to coordinate the wishes and efforts of family members. The step-by-step instructions for making and implementing care plans provide invaluable support for caregivers. I wish it had been available when I was caring for my own parents through their last illnesses."

—Leslie J. Harris, Dorothy Kliks Fones Professor of Law, University of Oregon

Life:
The Next Phase

Life: The Next Phase

NAVIGATING THE ISSUES OF CARING FOR YOUR AGING PARENTS OR LOVED ONES

MARY BETH
COZZA

HELEN B.
HEMPEL

JODI
HEMPEL

Life: The Next Phase
By Mary Beth Cozza, Helen B. Hempel, and Jodi Hempel

1. Family & Relationships/Reference FAM038000 2. Family & Relationships/ Eldercare FAM017000 3. Family & Relationships/Life Stages/Later Years FAM005000

ISBN 13: 978-1-935953-62-3
ISBN-10: 1935953621

Cover design by Marc Cozza, CO Projects

Printed in the United States of America

Authority Publishing
11230 Gold Express Dr. #310-413
Gold River, CA 95670
www.AuthorityPublishing.com
800-877-1097

AUTHORITY
PUBLISHING

DEDICATION

This book is dedicated to our family, friends and loved ones who have experienced or are experiencing the challenges of aging in a complex world. In addition, Mary Beth dedicates this book to her aunt and uncle, Mary and Rocco Dominicis. Jodi dedicates it in honor of her mother, Elsie Hempel. Helen dedicates it in honor of her husband, Val Hempel. Their courage, love and commitment to life have inspired us to take on this project and make a difference in the world.

MANY THANKS

We would like to thank several individuals who helped us in the creation and production of this book. First, thanks to Debbie Richardson, a dear friend, who came up with the title of the book. We'd also like to acknowledge Marc Cozza and Rebecca Cohen, CO Projects, for their talent and creativity in designing the book cover and photographs. Special thanks to Gail Nickel-Kailing, our editor, for her dedication and editing skills. And finally, thanks to Stephanie Chandler and her team at Authority Publishing. We sincerely appreciate these talented and dedicated individuals for helping us to bring our vision for this book to life.

CONTENTS

INTRODUCTION

Life is an opportunity, benefit from it. Life is beauty, admire it. Life is a dream, realize it. Life is a challenge, meet it. Life is a duty, complete it. Life is a game, play it. Life is a promise, fulfill it. Life is sorrow, overcome it. Life is a song, sing it. Life is a struggle, accept it. Life is a tragedy, confront it. Life is an adventure, dare it. Life is luck, make it. Life is too precious, do not destroy it. Life is life, fight for it.

—Mother Teresa

Your parent or loved one is one of the people that you care the most about; you want the very best for them—to be happy, healthy, engaged in life and, of course, safe. You have a finite amount of time to spend with your loved one, time that you cannot get back if you waste it, and you want your time together to be the highest quality, no matter the situation.

The goal of **Life: The Next Phase** is to give you best practices and tools so that you can help your parent or loved one have the highest quality of life for them, in their situation. Learn how to collaborate with your loved one to help him or her articulate their wishes for the remaining phase of their life. Become their partner and help carry out their wishes, instead of reversing roles and becoming their parent.

By helping you navigate the most common issues of caring for or assisting your loved one through the three major situations that seniors tend to encounter, this book will help you care for them without losing yourself in the process.

NOTE: You can use this book to navigate the issues faced by your parents or any other loved one, whether that is a spouse, partner, sibling, grandparent, aunt or uncle, mother- or father-in-law, or a dear friend. For ease of use, from here on we will use the term "loved one" to represent any of these relationships.

As your loved one ages, he or she may face issues making them unable to live independently. This can be a scary time for you both. It is difficult to see the people you love age and realize that they will not be with you forever. You want the best for them and you want to help them, so their issues become your issues.

The problem is that most of us have not gone through this before and don't know what to do or how to do it. So, you might do what you have done in other areas of your life where you have been successful: step in, take charge, make decisions, and get it handled.

And this is how the role reversal begins. You may think you are helping, but your loved one becomes defensive and resentful for being treated like a child. If you find that you take on more than you have the time and energy to do, you may feel resentful too. And then you feel guilty for feeling resentful. Instead of enjoying the time you spend with your loved one or parent, during the time they have left on this earth, your relationship becomes strained and the time spent is more of a chore than a joy.

If this is you, you are not alone, even though you may feel that way sometimes. The number of people in the U.S. over the age of 65 is expected to grow radically, from 40 million in 2010 to 55 million in 2020 to as many as 73 million in 2030. And the majority will need assistance and care from family and friends at some point in their lives.

Why should you read our book? Because we can help. Helen Hempel is certified as an Elder Law Attorney by the National Elder Law Foundation and has over 20 years experience as a private elder law practitioner. By the time she returned to school as a law student, Helen had had a number of careers, none of which had satisfied her, and she was a generation older than her fellow classmates.

During an apprenticeship to a woman who had a general practice with an emphasis on serving older clients, Helen observed what her mentor did in her practice and decided that elder law, then just a burgeoning specialty, was right for her. She knew the issues that occurred with aging, she could relate to older persons, and she wanted to ensure that the rights of seniors were protected.

Since then Helen has handled several thousand cases and has seen a wide variety of situations. She has a reputation for successfully resolving difficult cases—those that no one else wants. In addition to helping people through her practice, Helen and her sister assisted their parents as they went through the aging process.

Mary Beth Cozza's aunt, Mary, and uncle, Rocky, are both experiencing serious health issues at age 82 and 85. Rocky has Parkinson's disease and Mary has had chronic health issues throughout her life and recently broke her hip. Both of them need a full-time caregiver.

As they work through the maze of legal, financial, and medical complexity, Mary Beth provides support for her aunt, uncle and cousin. She is deeply motivated to make a difference and has chosen to use the skills she gained in the corporate world, where she worked as an executive leading organizational change, culture, and human resources to create tools and resources that support those caring for aging loved ones.

When Jodi Hempel was 19 years old, her mother, Elsie, had a massive stroke that left her unable to care for herself—a crisis for which neither was prepared. Jodi had to learn how to get her mother full-time care and rehabilitative therapy. She went through the process of becoming Elsie's conservator so she could handle her financial affairs.

Elsie improved and went on to live another 20 years during which time she was able to live independently, but due to other crises spent the last three years of her life under full-time care again. As an only child, Jodi understands what it is to be the sole support for someone and wants to help others handle situations similar to those with which she had to deal, and to avoid some of the mistakes she made.

We have pooled our collective experience and knowledge and designed a Roadmap that addresses the most common issues that your loved one is likely to encounter. We've applied that Roadmap to several different situations. As advocates and caregivers, we have learned what works and what doesn't. We have spent countless hours researching and interviewing people to learn the best ways to handle these situations so that you don't have to.

How to Use Life: The Next Phase

Life: The Next Phase is designed to be a guidebook or reference book. It is not intended to be read cover-to-cover, although you can if you choose. There are four sections that cover different situations that your loved one may be facing, and you may skip to the section that applies to your situation right now without having to read through pages that may not apply or be relevant to you. If your loved one's situation changes, read the section that applies to the new conditions.

The first three sections address these situations: your loved one needs some assistance some of the time to safely manage their day-to-day life; he or she is unable to safely live alone without a significant amount of assistance or supervision; or they are in the middle of a crisis: for example, a heart attack, stroke, or a fall with serious injuries. Each of these three sections begins with a real-life story illustrating the situation and the application of the Roadmap. If you have the benefit of time, you and/or your loved one can use the fourth section to put a comprehensive plan in place *today*, before the need arises.

There are two additional sections to this book. **Other Considerations** contains additional advice on issues like managing the people that provide assistance to your loved one, selecting a home health care professional, assisted living facility or nursing home, and talking with your loved one about driving. The final section, **Resources**, contains a list of other resources to help you. There are more resources than we could cover in this book, so we have provided relevant websites and other books to assist you to find resources, information, and support in your loved one's community.

This book is a lot of things, but there are several things that it is not. As we have said, it is not designed to be read cover to cover. There is some information repeated in each of the sections. For example, Step Four contains similar information across each section since the information applies to each situation in the same way. This was done intentionally to minimize the time you need to spend flipping back and forth between sections.

This book is also not all about *you*. We have purposely included very little information (although there is some) to help YOU with YOUR issues as you deal with your parents or loved one. This book is to help you partner with your loved ones; to help them with their issues, not to become their parents. They may not be as independent as they once were, they may need assistance and be child-like but they are not your children. Your loved one is an adult with extensive life experience and he or she deserves your respect. Your role, should you choose to accept it, is to understand and honor their wishes. To help him or her to live the most independent life they can according to their wishes, not yours.

You may have noticed in the situations that this book covers that we do not mention end of life or dying. We do not cover it in this book other than by addressing health-care directive and estate-planning documents such as wills and trusts.

The book does not contain a planning guide with worksheets. Please visit our website, Life: The Next Phase (www.lifethenextphase.com) to learn how to get our planning guide.

Assisting and caring for your aging parent or loved one is not easy, and this book is not a magic bullet or "Easy Button." It will help you and your loved one navigate the most common issues, but it will still require work from both of you.

The rewards, though, are priceless—knowing that your loved one is living the highest quality of life possible, knowing that you have done your part to help them do it, and to enjoy spending whatever time you have together.

Enjoy your journey through this phase
of your loved one's life!

GETTING STARTED
THE ROADMAP

"The truth is you and I are in control of only two things, how we prepare for what might happen, and how we respond to what just happened."

—DeVon Franklin

Your Starting Point

What is going on that is prompting you to read this book? Answering this question will point you to the section in this book that most applies to you and your loved one's situation.

Have you observed that things are different with them and you wonder if they are struggling with certain aspects of their life? If you answered yes, read the section of the book titled *When They Need Part-Time Assistance* next.

Has your loved one reached a point where they can no longer care for themselves or live independently and need 24-hour care and/or supervision? If you answered yes to this question, read the section titled *When They Need Full-Time Assistance*.

Is your loved one dealing with a crisis situation (which in turn is creating a crisis for you)? If you answered yes to this question, read the section called *When a Crisis Hits.*

Or are you being proactive and want to make sure that preparations are in place for what might happen in the future? In this case read the *Preparing for What Might Happen* section.

The Roadmap

Each of the four sections comprises a seven-step Roadmap that walks you through the issues and actions that you and your loved one should be considering.

Step 1. Having a Conversation with Your Loved One. The Roadmap will guide you through having conversations with your loved one to understand their wishes for this phase of their life, and doing that in such a way that they don't find the situation distressing.

Step 2. A Care Assessment. The Roadmap will help you and your loved one identify the areas where they need or want assistance.

Step 3. A Financial Assessment. The Roadmap will help you and your loved one put together a financial plan for covering immediate expenses as well as preparing for the rest of their life.

Step 4. Document Assessment and Inventory. The Roadmap will help you and your loved one gather and execute documents that will express their wishes and authorize their chosen representative to help them when such assistance may be needed.

Step 5. Maintaining Wellbeing. The Roadmap will guide you as you identify activities, networks, and tools to help your loved one create or maintain mental, physical, and emotional wellbeing in their life. These are things that are important to them and that keep them passionate about their lives; even if those lives have to take a different form during this phase.

Step 6. Create the Plan. At the end of each section is an "Action Planning Guide" so that you and your loved one can create a custom plan for your unique situation.

Step 7. Execute the Plan. Review often.

Now that you have determined what section or sections of the book will help you with your situation, let's get started!

WHEN THEY NEED
PART-TIME ASSISTANCE

Too often we underestimate the power of a touch, a smile, a kind word, a listening ear, an honest compliment, or the smallest act of caring, all of which have the potential to turn life around.

—Leo Buscaglia

Thelma and Silvia: Their Story

At 73, Silvia became terminally ill with chronic myeloid leukemia (CML), and she expressed a desire to live independently as long as possible. She was able to do so because of the commitment, dedication, and creativity of her family, including Thelma and her siblings. They joined together and used each other's talents to support Silvia no matter what obstacle came up.

As Silvia dealt with her illness, she went through seven different chemotherapy treatments. She was considered a "poster child," willing to try experimental drugs and designer therapies, even those with terrible side effects, to keep living. Her treatment was extremely expensive, at one point costing $3,000 a month.

Fortunately, years ago when she was still healthy, Silvia had wisely enrolled in a Medicare supplemental insurance plan that covered prescriptions. Her medical expenses, including the designer drugs that were used to help her keep her illness at bay, were covered completely through Medicare and the supplemental insurance. It was a one-time opportunity and luckily for her it later paid off.

For a period of time Silvia did get caught in the Medicare prescription "donut hole"—the Medicare Part D Coverage Gap—where her initial prescription coverage stopped and she had not yet reached the catastrophic coverage threshold. Because she couldn't afford to pay the additional expense for her chemo drugs, her children pitched in and covered it for her. It was hard for Silvia to accept the help because she prized being independent and self-sufficient.

At the recommendation of Silvia's sister-in-law, Thelma discovered that Silvia was eligible for TRICARE, a medical insurance plan for members of the armed forces, retirees, and their families, since her husband was a veteran of the Navy Reserves. TRICARE became the secondary payee covering whatever the supplemental insurance didn't pay.

Because the mortgage on her home was paid by a mortgage-protection insurance policy on her husband's death, Silvia could continue to live at home on Social Security and a small survivor's benefit from her husband's military pension.

As her illness progressed and Silvia became physically unable to manage her household on her own, Thelma asked a home health agency for recommendations on tools, technology, and services that would make it possible for Silvia to stay there: cell phone, medical alert system, housekeeping help, lawn care services, etc.

Thelma found affordable resources that fit with her mother's lifestyle. For example, she set up auto-pay for her bills so that her mother could keep track of the transactions and know where her money was going, and to give Silvia some feeling of control.

Silvia's willingness to honestly and openly let her children know what was happening made it easy for them to support her as needed. Most of Silvia's children lived close by and Thelma kept close watch on her mother so they were always able to help.

Then a few years later, the family noticed that Silvia was starting to forget and lose things. There were four or five episodes of her losing keys or her wallet. One time, in a panic, she called the police when she couldn't find her wallet and thought she had been pick-pocketed. Thelma talked with Silvia's doctor, who diagnosed mild-to-moderate dementia.

Thelma contacted a social worker to learn more and to find out what to do. The social worker coached Thelma and her siblings on ways to communicate with Silvia in simple terms and not to expect her to do anything too difficult. At the time Silvia was still driving and would not be able to continue when the dementia got worse. Her family wanted her to be able to stay independent because that was so important to her.

So they collaborated behind the scenes and someone talked to Silvia or stopped in to see her every day, and the family constantly conferred with each other about how they found her if something seemed amiss. They worked consistently with Silvia's doctors and nurses, who were available by phone and email.

Thelma and her siblings did whatever they could to help their mother interact and stay in contact with her friends and extended family. They arranged luncheons with close family members, and Thelma often took Silvia to see her great-granddaughter. Her Spanish family friends came and sang to her, as did her two great-grandsons—she was often surrounded by those who loved her.

Because Silvia's children had a strong and loving relationship with their mother and didn't judge her, they were able to gracefully work through a variety of situations, while still letting their mother stay in control of her life. Thelma was the point person; she kept everyone informed, and she collected questions from her siblings and emailed them to Silvia's doctors to get answers throughout her illness.

What if, at some point, Silvia could no longer live alone? How would the family support her? Thelma's sister from Hawaii even offered to come and live with their mother if needed. Together Thelma and her sisters met to devise a care plan in which they could all participate. "We all knew our mother's wishes, so everyone was aligned with the plan."

Introduction

You go home for the holidays and notice that things are not like they usually are; you are only there for a few days and feel pressure to "fix" everything before you leave. You are concerned that your loved one is having difficulty living on his or her own. Or you call your sister on the phone and she sounds confused; you panic thinking that she has had a stroke. Or your close friend mentions that he forgot to turn off the stove and left it on all night; you are thankful the house did not burn down. These are just some of the ways that it becomes clear our loved ones may need assistance.

Aging seniors have a strong desire to remain independent and in control of their lives for as long as possible. At some point, however, they may reach a time in their lives when they are unable to do some things for themselves. Usually, they will not be the one to tell you that they have reached this point; they may not want to admit that they need help and they don't want to be a burden to others. Your loved one is probably no different.

Because of his or her wish to remain independent and reluctance to discuss the situation, it is important that you and others watch for signs that your loved one needs help. Watch for things that may be different or changed: the house is disorderly when it was always neat before. You see unpaid bills lying around, laundry undone, the yard is overgrown and not maintained. Or you notice that your loved one hasn't been driving or that there are new dents in his car. The kitchen pantry is bare, you see she has lost weight or isn't eating well. What you observe will give you an idea of how much and what kind of assistance is needed.

Even though you may be tempted to jump in, take control, and do what you think is best, resist the urge! It is extremely important at this stage that a plan is put in place first—and that it is done with the input and consent of your loved one so they can remain in control of their life. And remember that even if they need help with some things, that does not necessarily mean they need help with everything. It is just as important to know what they can continue to do on their own as it is to know where they need help.

In this section, we apply situation-specific information to the Roadmap introduced in the Getting Started section and identify the actions to take when your loved one is showing signs that some assistance is needed to maintain their independence. To review, the seven steps of the Roadmap are:

1. Have a conversation with your loved one to understand their wishes.

2. Conduct a care needs assessment to determine the kinds of care needed.

3. Conduct a financial assessment to determine what resources are available.

4. Conduct a document assessment and inventory.

5. Ensure that your loved one maintains wellbeing.

6. Create a plan.

7. Execute and review the plan.

As Silvia's illness progressed, Thelma observed that her mother was physically unable to manage her household on her own and that she needed some assistance. Thelma and her siblings implemented the Roadmap in caring for their mother. Here's how they did it:

1. Have a conversation with your loved one to understand their wishes: *Thelma found helping her mother easy because Silvia was willing to honestly and openly let Thelma know what was happening.*

2. Conduct a care needs assessment: *Thelma had a home health agency come to Silvia's home and make recommen-*

dations on how to make the house safer and more accessible to her mother.

3. Conduct a financial assessment: *Thelma discovered that her mother had both Medicare and supplemental insurance that included prescription benefits. She later found that Silvia was also eligible for TRICARE because her husband had been in the military.*

4. Conduct a document inventory: *Thelma found that Silvia's mortgage was paid off because her late husband had purchased insurance to cover it in the event of either spouse's death.*

5. Maintain loved one's wellbeing: *Thelma and her siblings helped their mother stay in touch with friends and extended family. They arranged luncheons with close family members and often took Silvia to see her great-granddaughter.*

6. Create a plan: *Thelma and her sisters met with Silvia to come up with a care plan in which they could all participate.*

7. Execute and review the plan: *Thelma was the point person and kept everyone informed as to how the plan was working.*

Step 1: Having a Conversation with Your Loved One

We can't stress enough how important it is to involve your loved one in getting the support and care that they need; start by having conversations with them! The purpose of having open and supportive conversations is to help your loved one recognize and accept that they need assistance in certain areas of their life, for you to learn their wishes, and to gain their acceptance of the help. Unless their safety is at risk and something needs to be addressed immediately, there can be several conversations over a period of time. The first conversation may be to just introduce the subject. The second may be to learn their wishes. A third may be to explore options.

The first goal of the conversations is to determine what is important in four main categories: finances, home, activities, and work.

- **Finances**: Help them identify their goals for their finances: for example, do they want to be as financially independent as possible, to have a safety fund in the event of emergency or crisis, or to buy a second home?

- **Home**: With regard to your loved one's home, how does she want to live: does she want to remain in her own home for as long as possible, to live close to family, to relocate to another city, or downsize to a smaller home?

- **Activities**: What kind of activities does he want to do to remain healthy and active: pursue a hobby or take classes, be involved in the community or do volunteer/ charity work, travel, or be involved with his family and grandchildren?

- **Work**: If your loved one is still working, what are their wishes: for example, do they want to work as long as possible, do they want to retire soon, or do they want to start a new business?

The second goal is to gain their acceptance of the fact that they need help with certain things. Discussing what is getting in the way of meeting their goals and fulfilling their wishes will begin to bring up areas where they see that they need help.

Planning the Conversations

Your first conversation should be one-on-one with your loved one. This is not the time to stage a family (or group) intervention; they need to feel that it is safe to have this discussion. The results from your first conversation will determine whether or not the follow-up conversations should also be one-on-one or whether the family or others should be involved. The determining factor is whether or not he or she is willing to accept help. If they are, then suggest bringing the family/group together to start the planning—and get his or her approval. On the other hand, if they do not accept that they need help or they do not give you approval to bring in others, keep the conversations one-on-one until you get their acceptance and approval.

Broaching the subject may be something that neither you nor your loved one really wants to do, especially if they have been extremely independent. For this reason, before you have any conversation, do some preparation. Who is the best person to have the initial discussion? It might be you, or it might be someone else. For example, if you are planning a conversation with your father and he still thinks of you as a child who should listen to authority and not talk back, you probably are not the best person to have this conversation. A trusted friend and advisor may be better suited. On the other hand, if your loved one often looks to you for advice, you might be the best person for the job. Discuss your concerns with other family members and/or friends to get agreement and to decide who should have the conversation.

Take some time to think about *your* concerns for the conversation and try to minimize them. What will you do if they get angry, cry, or clam up and won't talk? Preparing for—and even rehearsing—these scenarios will make them less stressful. Talk with family/friends in advance about the kind of support they are able and willing to provide, if any, so you know what is possible and what you can offer during the conversation.

Make the conversation convenient for your loved one. Pick a day and time that works with his or her schedule. Select a place where they will be comfortable, where the sound level is such that you can easily converse and they can hear you, and where you have privacy without concern of being overheard.

Approach the conversation with an open mind; do not have any preconceived ideas about where the conversation will go or the outcome. Remember: your purpose for the conversation is to focus on your loved one's needs, safety, and wellbeing.

Having the Conversations

Ask for permission to discuss the topic. Perhaps you would be comfortable starting off sharing something that you have observed like, *I noticed that the house is not tidy as it usually is. Can we talk about that?* Or if the time is appropriate you could say, *I'd like to talk about your wishes for your life so that I can partner with you to make sure that happens. Can we do that now?*

Once you start the conversation, listen to what your loved one is saying without interrupting, giving your opinion, or telling him or her what to do. To be sure that you have a clear understanding of what they have said, periodically repeat back to them in your own words what you've heard your loved one say to you. Pay just as much attention to what's not being said as what is being said—observe their facial expressions, gestures, posture, and other nonverbal clues.

Start at a high level. Begin by asking general open-ended questions; then you can go further with follow-up questions on areas of concern. For example, you could start with, *How have you been feeling lately?* Based on the answer, you might follow with more detailed questions.

Rather than offer advice, let them work things out for themselves as they talk. Explore the situation by asking open-ended, non-threatening questions like, *What is most important to you? What specifically concerns you?* or *How do you feel about that?*

Bring up "what if" scenarios. You can ask things like, *What if you couldn't get up and down the stairs anymore? What if you couldn't drive anymore? What if you suddenly needed help with certain activities of daily living? What would your wishes be if you could no longer live at home without assistance?*

You can refer to what friends or other family members have done as a conversation starter. For example, *What did you think of Aunt Mary moving into an assisted living facility?* Your loved one may have very strong opinions about someone else's situation and either agree or not with their choices. Talking about other's choices may help them understand their own wishes better. Or you may talk about any planning that you are doing for yourself, for example, *Bob and I are planning to downsize to a small condo once the kids are in college. We just don't want to have to take care of that big house any more at that point.*

Be honest and direct. Do not cover up or avoid talking about what they might think of as negative information. Don't make promises you might not be able to keep like, *We'll never put you in a nursing home,* or *You can always come and live with us, we'll take care of you.* Circumstances change over time and what may seem like the best solution now may not be the best solution years from now. Unfulfilled promises can only result in extreme guilt, anxiety, and pain. Instead, let your loved one know that you will keep his or her wishes in mind and do your best to help fulfill them providing it can be done safely.

Throughout the conversations, tell them how much you love them, how important these conversations are, and how you're willing to work with them to find answers to these tough questions.

This is a lot to take on in one sitting, so it's recommended that you have several conversations over time on this subject. Perhaps you live out of town or are very busy yourself and you're worried about what could happen if you don't have this all figured out right now. Don't try to force it all in one visit; it's a progression of change over time. Most importantly, understand what their wishes are so you can assess available options to address the situation.

Step 2: A Care Assessment—
Getting the Help Needed

In the context of a care assessment, "help" refers to the many services that provide non-medical and/or medical care for someone who cannot provide the care for him or herself. In general, people require three types of assistance:

- **Self-care**: Eating, walking, bathing, dressing, toilet, or transferring—from bed to wheelchair

- **Living assistance**: Light housework, preparing meals, taking medications, shopping for groceries or clothes, using the telephone, and managing money

- **Professional healthcare**: Medical or psychological assessment, wound care, medication training, pain management, disease education and management, physical therapy, speech therapy, or occupational therapy

The first step is to determine the level and type of assistance needed; your loved one will need assistance with things they can no longer do on their own or do safely. Assistance is not necessarily needed just because they do things more slowly, differently than they used to, or differently than you would. Assistance is help needed to do what they *cannot* do any longer or *should* not do for safety reasons. It is recommended that you observe them doing certain tasks to see whether or not they need assistance.

If you need help conducting a needs assessment you can contact a geriatric care manager (also known as elder care manager, senior healthcare manager, or professional care manager). A geriatric care manager helps individuals and families adjust and cope with the challenges of aging or disability. They can conduct a care planning assessment to identify needs, problems, and eligibility for assistance. A physician can also help with medical and psychological assessments. Refer to *Choosing a Geriatric*

Care Manager in the **Other Considerations** section of this book for additional information.

Step 3: A Financial Assessment— Determine What Resources Are Available

Once you know the kind and level of care that's needed, you may find that it is beyond what family/friends can provide or can be provided free of charge. If your loved one needs to use services that require payment or a change in living arrangements, you need to help them determine how they will pay for it in addition to their other expenses. It is ideal if they planned for this eventuality well in advance of needing care, at a time when they had the greatest number of options to consider. Conduct a careful financial assessment with your loved one to determine and document income, assets, insurance, and debts so you both have a clear and complete financial picture.

Own Assets/Current Income

Many services, like bringing in a housekeeper or moving to an assisted living facility are considered non-medical services, and are therefore not covered by insurance or government programs. If your loved one needs these services, he or she will need to have the money to pay for them, so it's extremely important to know what assets and income sources are available. The following are some options:

Social Security. Most likely your loved one is eligible for Social Security. Social Security helps, but it probably is not enough on its own. The Social Security Administration's website (www.ssa. gov) has information and interactive tools. An account can be set up and benefit information viewed online.

Primary Home. If your loved one owns his or her home and has equity in it, the home may be a source of income, either through an equity loan, reverse mortgage, rental, or sale.

- **Equity Loan.** Your loved one may be able to borrow against the equity in his or her home to provide money to pay for expenses. This is a viable option *if* they plan to continue to own the home *and* have the ability to make the payments on the equity loan.

- **Reverse Mortgage.** For someone who wants to remain living at home, a reverse mortgage on a primary residence may be an option to generate income. The name "reverse mortgage" describes exactly what it is. The homeowner, upon qualifying for a reverse mortgage, receives payments instead of making payments.

Because there are costs—sometimes considerable—for qualifying for and obtaining a reverse mortgage, it is an option appropriate only for someone who will be able to live at home for five years or more, a common benchmark. These costs can include a loan-origination fee, appraisal fee, third-party closing costs, and a mortgage insurance premium. Borrowers who cannot pay these costs directly can finance them through the reverse mortgage.

To qualify for a reverse mortgage, homeowners must be 62 or older and remain living in the home. There are no income requirements for a reverse mortgage, but the recipient(s) must be able to continue to pay property taxes, insurance, and upkeep on the property.

If the homeowner becomes ill, is hospitalized, and later must spend time in a nursing home, absences of less than a year are permitted. However, if the homeowner is out of the home for a year or more, then the mortgage will be due and payable.

Similarly, when the homeowner dies, the reverse mortgage must be repaid. How much equity, if any, is left at that point depends upon the amount of money paid from the loan, the interest rate, and any home appreciation. Usually, the home is sold and the mortgage is paid. If the loan balance due is less than the value of the house, the difference is paid to the heirs. It is important to note that neither the homeowner nor the heirs will ever owe more than the current value of the home at the time the home is sold or the loan paid, even if the value of the home has declined.

Payments to the homeowner from a reverse mortgage can be made in a variety of forms. The homeowner can receive a lump sum, monthly payments, or establish a line of credit; some lenders provide a combination of these payment forms. The important thing to remember is that reverse mortgages should be used for their intended purpose: that is, to provide care or assistance to enable a senior to remain living at home.

There are, however, no restrictions on how funds from a reverse mortgage can be used. And, unfortunately, there have been instances where borrowers have taken money from a reverse mortgage to buy luxury items or take "a trip of a lifetime" and afterward did not have enough remaining to pay for necessities.

- **Rent or Sell.** If your loved one must move out of their home, they may be able to rent or sell the home to generate additional funds.

Additional Real Estate. If your loved one owns a vacation home or investment property, they may be able to borrow against it, get rental income, or sell the property.

Other resources. There may be additional resources set aside, such as an IRA, pension fund, or other qualified plan. Consider the distribution schedule and various distribution options, and, do not forget to take into account the tax consequences of distribution.

What other resources are available? Does your loved one have bank accounts, mutual funds, stocks and/or bonds? Do they receive income from a trust? Can those payments be increased? What about a pension or an annuity? Regardless of the resource, always stop to assess the tax consequences of any of the financial decisions you make.

Outside Sources

One of the largest expenses a senior has is medical and other healthcare costs. A couple retiring in 2013 at the age of 65 can expect to pay an average of $220,000 for healthcare costs, according to a study by Fidelity Benefits Consultants. This amount includes approximately 20 years of costs (into their early to mid-eighties), and consists of insurance payments, co-payments, prescription drugs, doctor visits, and other expenses that Medicare doesn't cover. It does not include over-the-counter medications, dental care, and long-term care. It is important to know the resources your loved one has available and what each covers—and doesn't cover.

Medicare. The first thing to consider when paying for healthcare is Medicare. It is governmental medical insurance and pays for most visits to the doctor, preventive care, hospital outpatient, hospital inpatient, laboratory tests, x-rays, and mental healthcare. It also may provide coverage for prescription drugs and some ambulance fees.

Some people wrongly assume that Medicare, Medicare supplemental policies, or standard health insurance policies will cover the costs of long-term care, whether that care is provided in the home, in an assisted living residence, or a nursing home. They don't. As a result, people often fail to plan and are then dismayed to learn of their mistake when services are needed. For more information on Medicare coverage, go to the Medicare website at: www.medicare.gov.

Private-pay Medical Insurance. Your loved one may also have private insurance or supplemental insurance; if so, refer to the policy to determine exactly what is covered. Make a note of the cost of the premiums as a debt/expense.

Long-Term Care Insurance. Long-term care insurance is intended to cover the cost of care at home or in a facility, for individuals whose chronic disabilities make independent living impossible. Those disabilities may be physical or cognitive. Long-term care insurance does not cover medical care or short-term care such as rehabilitation following an illness or hospitalization.

If your loved one has already purchased a long-term care policy, it may defray the cost of home health services or the cost of living in a facility. However, once a health crisis has occurred, purchasing long-term care insurance is no longer an option; the policy holder must be in a good health at the time the insurance policy is issued.

Veterans Administration. If your loved one is a veteran or is the spouse of a deceased veteran, he or she may be entitled to benefits. Veteran's benefits may include a pension, healthcare, and nursing home or assisted living facilities. Check with his or her local or regional Veterans Affairs Office to see if they qualify. There are organizations that can help navigate the VA; some are free, others charge a fee for their services. To access the Veterans Affairs website, go to www.va.gov. To locate an organization to assist you, do an Internet search for "assistance with VA benefits."

Medicaid. For older persons who have limited income and resources, Medicaid is a needs-based program available to pay for medical costs and a variety of services not covered by Medicare. The funds for this program are provided jointly by the federal government and by state governments, and the services vary state by state. Depending upon the state in which you live, Medicaid dollars can be used for long-term care in the home or in a facility.

In order to qualify for Medicaid, there are both income and resource limitations. Those limitations also vary from state to state, although the federal government, through the Centers for Medicare and Medicaid Services, sets eligibility standards and limits as to what assets your loved one can own and still be eligible for Medicaid. For married couples, if only one spouse needs Medicaid, the other spouse can live at home or in a facility other than a nursing home and is permitted to keep enough assets to enable them to live independently. As demand for long-term care has risen, stricter rules have been made to ensure that people do not purposely impoverish themselves by giving their assets away for the purpose of qualifying for Medicaid. And, if those applying for Medicaid have given away their assets, they will be penalized by not being eligible to receive benefits.

When recipients of Medicaid die, the state may seek reimbursement for the benefits that they have received. Generally, anything that the Medicaid recipient owned on the date of death is potentially available for recovery by the state. For example, if the Medicaid recipient's name was left on any asset (most commonly seen on a deed) then the state may claim the Medicaid recipient's share of the asset. This doesn't refer to assets that were legitimately transferred, whether sold or given away, only to something on which the Medicaid recipient's name remains. For information on Medicaid in your loved one's state go to www.medicaid.gov.

Debt Assessment

Once you know the sources of income, determine all debts and projected expenses including mortgage or rent payments, insurance premiums, utilities, other loan payments, necessities, and entertainment. This will give you an accurate picture of how many funds you have available.

Step 4: Document Inventory and Assessment

A document inventory will provide a clear and complete picture of all documents in place to protect your loved one as he or she ages. It is important to have the following documents in place *before* they are needed.

Documents That Every Adult Should Have

- **Durable Power of Attorney for Healthcare**: Enables your loved one to appoint someone to make healthcare decisions on their behalf if they cannot make the decisions for themselves.

- **Advanced Healthcare Directive**: Includes a durable power of attorney for healthcare as well as a statement of wishes for end-of-life care.

- **Living Will**: Allows your loved one to state the type of healthcare they want and do not want at the end of their life.

- **Power of Attorney**: Allows your loved one to appoint someone to make financial decisions and financial transactions on their behalf. A durable power of attorney remains effective even if the person loses capacity.

- **Will:** States how assets should be distributed when your loved one dies. In most states, this distribution requires court involvement.

- **Living Trust**: States how your loved one's assets will be managed during his or her lifetime, who should take over management if he or she becomes incapacitated, and how their assets are to be distributed at the time of death. Usually there is no court involvement.

If these documents are not in place and the need for them arises, you will likely need to hire an attorney and go to court to get authority to make healthcare and financial decisions for your loved one. This can be both time-consuming and costly. See *Documents Every Adult Should Have* in the **Other Considerations** section of this book for more information to help you determine which documents are needed.

Personal and Business Documents

The last step in planning is to make an inventory of various personal and business documents, account numbers, policy numbers, and locations, to simplify access when you or someone else needs it in the future. The list includes but is not limited to:

- Bank names and account number(s),
- Birth certificates,
- Brokerage firm names and account numbers,
- Deeds on real estate owned,
- Divorce decrees,
- Education and employment records,
- Insurance policies (including company names and policy numbers),
- Maiden name (if applicable),
- Marriage certificates,
- Medicare card and number,
- Military discharge papers,
- Mortgage documents,
- Passports,
- Pets' names and veterinarian's phone number,
- Religious affiliation and name of clergy,

- Social Security card and number,
- Spouse death certificates,
- Any other appropriate personal or business documents.

Step 5: Maintain Your Loved One's Wellbeing

Regardless of the level of assistance that is needed, it is important that your loved one maintains as high a quality of life as is possible: maintains mental, physical, and emotional wellbeing. Wellbeing is not available by prescription, and there is no one path—it is unique to each of us. A sense of wellbeing is a state of mind that depends not only on our thoughts, feelings, and actions, but also on what happens to us, the events and circumstances of our lives, and the genes and personality we were born with.

Depression and loneliness are very common in aging seniors, many times occurring when social circles change due to family and friends moving away or passing on, or when they lose their autonomy, because they have difficulty seeing, hearing, or walking. Obvious symptoms of depression are changing social patterns—they may stop going out, have difficulty sleeping, appetite loss, or a change in activities: for instance, they may stop reading or engaging in conversation.

Unfortunately, some discount the symptoms and describe the situation as, *They're just getting old.* Also, normal changes in the brain occur with aging; sometimes cognitive decline cannot be avoided, but in other cases, keeping the mind stimulated or interacting with others may help ward off isolation and depression. Certain illnesses such as Alzheimer's disease or other dementias can make it more difficult to learn new information or remember things.

Tips for Maintaining Wellbeing

There are many ways to stay socially connected and intellectually stimulated; the best options for your loved ones are those in which he or she can comfortably participate and that fit his or her interests.

Nurture a Social Network

It's important that seniors make an effort to maintain close personal relationships with family members, friends, members of their religious community, neighbors, and other important people in their lives. Even if they're not close by, technology like email, Skype, or Facebook can play a key role in keeping people connected. According to data from the Pew Research Center's *Internet & American Life Project,* the 74-plus demographic is the fastest-growing group across Web-based social networks. Use of sites like Facebook and Twitter among Internet users 65 and older grew 100 percent between 2009 and 2010, from 13 percent to 26 percent. Many assisted living centers have even begun offering technology classes to get seniors online and in the social-networking loop.

Join a Senior Community

Many cities and towns have senior centers that are set up for socializing and shared interests, so find out the location of the Senior Center nearest your loved one. Centers differ from community to community, but often have luncheons, dances, hobby groups, various lessons in different skills, etc. If you can, make it a point to drive your loved one to the Senior Center for events that they might find interesting. Often, they don't want to go because they don't know anyone; go with them a few times to help them to ease into the new community of acquaintances. Once they start making friends, they will feel more comfortable.

Play "Mind" Games

Regularly doing crossword puzzles and playing chess or other intellectually stimulating games keeps the mind active, and playing with others helps maintain social connections. Scientists believe that both the body and the mind follow the principle of "use it or lose it." So think of these games as fun ways to exercise the brain.

Join a Club

Find a club or group with a shared interest such as a weekly or monthly book club, garden club, or art club meetings. They are great ways to meet new people and develop rewarding relationships with people who have similar interests. Technology can help you find clubs with shared interests—conduct an Internet search on any club or group topic, and include the name of your city or neighborhood.

Go Back to Work

Many people experience stress after they retire or if illness changes their ability to live life as before. Some seniors are longing to work again. Finding a part-time job can help keep the mind stimulated and create a sense of greater contribution. Encore.org (formally Civic Ventures) and AARP's Work Search Program offer assistance to older people who want to get back into the workforce.

Volunteer in Your Community

Many people who want to have a feeling of purpose or contribute to a greater cause find it by volunteering in their community. Recent studies show that older individuals who volunteer have a reduced risk of premature death compared to their counterparts who do not. Local schools are always looking for volunteers to assist in the classroom, reading, arts and crafts, field trips, etc. You can also find out about volunteer opportunities through organizations like **Senior Corps**, a government-run organization that connects seniors with local and national organizations in need of volunteers.

Offer Family Assistance

If there are grandchildren or other young members in the family, babysitting or spending time with them offers support for the parents and creates ways to deepen family relationships. Chasing around after young children is a great way to keep physically active and to improve your sense of wellbeing.

Nurture the Body and Soul

How we feel both physically and emotionally impacts our level of wellbeing. Taking simple actions to nurture the body and spirit creates a connection to our hearts, allowing who we are at the core to continue. Here are some ways to nurture the body and soul:

- **Soothe the soles.** Foot massage, a non-invasive treatment, is highly beneficial and it helps to induce relaxation, which in turn aids the body's own healing processes. Massage can relieve the general aches and pains associated with getting older, and everyone deserves a little pampering, especially in their later years. Above all, it is perfect for those who can no longer get out and about, as a foot massage can be enjoyed from the comfort of a favorite armchair.

- **Exercise.** Many communities have exercise classes geared toward seniors, including chair exercise and yoga. And joining a class is a great way to expand the social circle too. As long as your loved one is physically able, he or she should be encouraged to continue to participate in the athletic pursuits they enjoyed when younger such as walking or hiking, skiing, cycling, or playing tennis.

- **Create gourmet delights**. Mealtimes are an important event in the day, and spending time on preparation and planning can be meaningful to many seniors. Sitting down at the start of the day and planning out the menu together or perusing cookbooks can add creativity and relationship-building to a normal everyday task. Many seniors have dietary restrictions and get tired of the same food day after day. There are many options and resources today to help make mealtime tasty and enjoyable.

- **Share a snapshot of life**. Getting out the family album and reminiscing is a great way for elders to reconnect with what is important to them and to stimulate favorite memories. Encourage them to take the lead in telling about various pictures; many seniors have travelled the world and can relive their journeys. Everyone has a story to tell and all of us enjoy remembering birthday celebrations and events with humorous anecdotes.

- **Music is food for the soul**. Music brings out many emotions, and being in touch with our feelings and working through them is as important at 95 as it is at 5. Indulging in a game of "Name That Tune" not only exercises the mind but brings joy and entertainment to the day.

- **Share experiences.** We all have our own favorite hobbies and pastimes and sharing these is an ideal way to get to know someone. It could be stamp collecting, coin collecting, or flower pressing.

- **Meditation**. Meditation yields numerous benefits for those young and old. Many older participants are reaping the benefits that meditation brings such as lowering blood pressure, relieving stress, clearing the mind, focusing memory, managing pain, and improving sleep.

Step 6: Creating the Plan

Once you know your loved one's wishes, the type of assistance that is needed, the resources available, and what has already been put in place, you can pull it all together and create a plan. Always involve your loved one in their own care—both knowledge of and consent for the plan—unless some form of mental or physical incapacity prevents them from participating.

Family and friends may be able to manage the assistance needed, but if not there are many services available. Here are some examples:

Need: Housecleaning and laundry.
Solution: Hire someone to come in every other week and clean the house, change the sheets on the bed and do the laundry.

Need: Grocery shopping.
Solution: Utilize a major grocery chain's online ordering and delivery service.

Need: Meal preparation.
Solution: Meals on Wheels or a similar service.

Need: Yard maintenance.
Solution: Hire a gardener to come in to mow the lawn and prune the bushes and trees. Install a sprinkler or drip system with a timer to water the garden and lawn.

Need: Taking medications on schedule.
Solution: Purchase a box with compartments for each day of the week. Once a week put medications in the corresponding compartment for each day and call daily to remind him or her to take the medication.

Need: Bathing.
Solution: Hire a home care professional to come in and assist.

According to the *Genworth Cost of Care Survey 2013,* the national median rates for care are as follows:

Service Provided	National Median Rate
Homemaker Services (Licensed): Provides "hands-off" care such as helping with cooking and running errands. Often referred to as "Personal Care Assistants" or "Companions."	$18/hour*
Home Health Aide Services (Licensed): Provides "hands-on" personal care, but not medical care, in the home, with activities such as bathing, dressing and transferring.	$19/hour*

*Rate charged by a non-Medicare certified licensed agency.

Refer to the tips for choosing a healthcare professional in the **Other Considerations** section.

If your loved one is going to remain living in his or her home, the home may need to be modified or retrofitted for safety and mobility. This will cost money, but most of such costs are minimal. Examples of modifications are the removal of throw rugs, and installation of stair railings, grab bars in showers and tubs, and sliding shelves in cabinets. Examples of retrofitting are installation of ramps, walk-in showers, and stair lifts.

In some cases, your loved one may want to make a change in their living arrangement. He or she may want to downsize from a large family home or move from a two-story house to avoid climbing stairs. One option for a change is an assisted living facility, which often encourages privacy but offers round-the-clock support and access to care. They offer help with things like cooking, housekeeping, and transportation to appointments, and some offer assistance with getting to the bathroom in the middle of the night or bathing.

Assisted living facilities come in all sizes, from a residential home with only a few residents to larger facilities with hundreds of residential units. A resident can start out living independently in their own apartment and add more care as it is needed. An assisted living facility may be a good option if there is a need for more assistance than family and friends are able to provide, if your loved one feels lonely at home, safety is a worry, transportation is an issue, or maintaining a home is too difficult. The average cost is $3,450 per month ($41,400 per year), which can be higher or lower depending on location.

Another option may be to combine households; your loved one might move in with a family member or friend or vice versa—a family member or friend might move in with them. Regardless of the choice, whenever two or more people are living together, communication is the key to success. Discuss potential issues up front, including who will pay for what, so that everyone has the same expectations—and to avoid misunderstandings and conflicts. To minimize issues later on, we recommend making a written plan that documents your understanding. Review your plans periodically to see if modifications need to be made.

Note: A Continuous Care Retirement Community is probably not an option for your loved one at this stage because most require that the resident be totally independent at the time they join the facility. And, a nursing home probably is not an option either since they offer a higher level of care than is needed at this stage.

Adjust Expenses

Can expenses be reduced? Money not spent on other things is money available to pay for assistance. Some expenses are fixed, such as a mortgage payment, but others are flexible. For example, there is more than one option for telephone and cable services and each has multiple plans. Some utility providers have special programs for seniors and/or low-income households. Changing credit card providers may lower interest rates. Depending on the circumstances, paying off the mortgage may free up monthly cash flow. Can you or family members contribute funds to your loved one's care?

Build a Support Team

Unless you will be the only person assisting your loved one's needs, assemble a team of people who can provide assistance. Your team may be made up of any combination of family members, friends, and people that have been hired to help. Refer to "Building a Support Team" in the **Other Considerations** section.

The Village

There is a new form of support that is starting to show up in cities across America; it is called the Village. A Village is not a place, but a set of support services that make it possible for someone to stay in their home. A nonprofit organization is formed, with a board of directors and staff or volunteers made up of people from the community. The services vary but can include referrals and discounts with vetted suppliers, transportation, home healthcare, help with household tasks, computer assistance, and social and educational activities. There is typically an annual fee that can range from $150 to $800 per person, which covers the administration of the Village. Some of the services provided may be included in the annual fee, and there may be additional fees for other services provided; this will vary from one Village to another. At the time of this writing, there are about 50 Villages up and running, the most well known being the Beacon Hill Village in Boston, MA. In addition, hundreds are in various stages of creation. Search online to see if there is a Village established in your loved one's community.

Documenting the Action Plan

All action plans will be different, but at the same time all contain the same kinds of information: the task or activity, the date and time it will take place, the name of the person responsible, and any notes. This is an example of a simple action plan.

Task/Activity	Date/Time	Point Person	Notes
Take Mom to meet with Attorney regarding documents	Monday, 10:00 am	Steve	Pick Mom up at 9:30
Contact the VA regarding benefits	Tuesday 9:00 am	Steve	
Grocery Shopping	Tuesday 5:30 pm	Mary	Get Mom's shopping list
Take out garbage cans	Wednesday 7:30 am	Tom	
House cleaning	Thursday 1:00 pm	ABC Housecleaning Service	
Knitting club	Friday 2:00	Friend Linda	
Take Mom to visit the Assisted Living Facility	Saturday at Noon	Mary	

Step 7: Executing and Reviewing the Plan

Now that you have a plan—execute it. If your plan has been carefully thought out, it may work without any tweaks or changes. But if it doesn't, review it, and make any necessary adjustments so that it does work. Just like your GPS, when something changes you need to recalculate; if something doesn't work or the situation changes, make adjustments until it works smoothly.

Even if your loved one is able to live independently, with assistance, for many years, we recommend that you review the plan together with them annually—or more frequently if other concerns arise—to make sure you are providing all of the support they need and keeping them safe. If your loved one reaches a point where they need around-the-clock care, see the next section **When They Need Full-time Assistance** for help in creating a plan for that stage.

Now that you have a plan for your loved one's current situation, you can relax and enjoy talking and spending time together.

We suggest that you read the other sections in this book to put plans in place so that if your loved one reaches the point that they need full-time assistance or if a crisis should arise, you will already have a plan in place.

Your Action Plan—A Checklist

Now that you have carefully read this section and followed the *7-Step Roadmap,* here is a summary of actions that you may use as a checklist to make sure you haven't missed anything.

1. Have a conversation with your loved one to determine their wants and needs.

    a. Finances

    b. Home

   c. Activities

   d. Work

2. Do a care assessment to determine where they need help.

   a. Self Care: Bathing, dressing, eating, walking, transferring.

   b. Living Assistance: Light housework, preparing meals, taking medications, shopping for groceries or clothes, using the telephone, managing money.

   c. Professional Healthcare: Medical or psychological assessment, wound care, medical instruction, pain management, disease education and management, physical therapy, speech therapy, occupational therapy.

3. Do a financial assessment to determine how to pay for the care they need.

   a. What outside sources do they currently have?

      i. Insurance: Medicare, private pay insurance, long-term care insurance, Veteran's Administration, Medicaid.

      ii. Assets: House, investments, rental property.

      iii. Monthly income and debts: Social Security, pension, mortgage, insurance premiums.

   b. Outside contributions from others, support from family members.

4. Determine what documents are in place and where they are located.

   a. Durable Power of Attorney

   b. Advanced Healthcare Directive

   c. Living Will

   d. Power of Attorney

   e. Will

   f. Living Trust

   g. Social Security number and card

   h. Military card/Service papers

   i. Insurance Policies

   j. Legal Documents

   k. Tax Returns

5. Ensure your loved ones' wellbeing.

   a. Nurture their social network

   b. Create activities to exercise the mind and body

   c. Join a senior community

   d. Join a club

   e. Go back to work

   f. Volunteer

   g. Offer family assistance

   h. Exercise

   i. Create family albums, look at family pictures and read to them

   j. Play music

   k. Meditation

6. Create the plan with your loved one using all the information you've collected.

   a. Some options:

      i. Housecleaning and laundry

      ii. Grocery shopping

      iii. Meal preparation

      iv. Yard maintenance

      v. Taking medications on schedule

      vi. Bathing

      vii. Home modifications and retrofitting

        viii. Continuing care retirement community

        ix. Assisted living facility

        x.   Combine households

    b. Create a budget

7. Execute and review the plan often.

WHEN THEY NEED FULL-TIME ASSISTANCE

When you do nothing, you feel overwhelmed and powerless. But when you get involved, you feel the sense of hope and accomplishment that comes from knowing you are working to make things better.

—Pauline R. Kezer

Jennifer and Rick: Their Story

In 2004, when Jennifer was overseas in the Peace Corps, she started noticing that something wasn't right with her dad, Rick, during their conversations. And when Rick came to visit, she noticed a different person. Rick had always been a highly professional, accomplished person, and now he was forgetful even with the simplest things and just couldn't focus.

Rick's career consisted of success as a salesperson, certified hypnotherapist, and a community activist. He had always been on top of things but now, at age 55, things were different. When Jennifer returned from the Peace Corps, she discovered her father had four months of unpaid bills, and had lost his ability to manage his finances and other responsibilities.

A medical evaluation and neuropsychological testing resulted in several diagnoses. The doctor determined that Rick was suffering from early-onset Alzheimer's, dementia, cognitive impairment, and aphasia, among other things. Her father had no job, no income, and lots of debt, so Jennifer was faced with limited options for her father's support.

Jennifer's first step was to become Rick's guardian and executor before the disease affected his ability to make decisions. Then, she worked on getting Rick on Social Security Disability. At the time there was an 18-month waiting period before benefits would start.

Next, Jennifer came up with alternative living situations for her father to try. She and her dad bought a house where she cared for him and worked. Jennifer didn't have any family members that could help her; she was on her own. When caring for Rick became more difficult, she hired caregivers to help.

Then it became obvious that Rick needed more care than Jennifer could provide at home, so she looked into assisted living facilities. Someone had referred her to a local facility, which is best described as one-stop shopping, where all his medical providers would be in one place. The facility also had contracts with various other facilities and residences to assist Rick as the disease progressed. He was assigned a social worker that took over his case-management at no cost. Rick's care cost $6,000 a month and Medicaid paid for the service. Although Rick was on Medicaid, Jennifer couldn't believe it was so expensive. What would she have done if Rick hadn't been eligible for Medicaid?

Rick had difficulties when he resided at the assisted living facility. Besides some issues with aggressive behavior, every time Jennifer came to visit, he would become very emotional and cling to her when she had to leave. The *situation was so distressing for Jennifer that she decided to quit her job and bring her father back home so she could provide him with comfortable surroundings, his pets, and friends nearby. She would learn how to make this work.*

Through the assisted living facility, Jennifer learned about her state's Relative Foster Home program and she became certified as a Relative Adult Foster Home Provider. To get the certification, Jennifer had to be able to care for Rick in a home that she owned and had to pass a criminal background check. The Department of Human Services performed an in-home inspection to evaluate the safety of the environment (fire alarms, etc.). Once she was certified as a Relative Adult Foster Home Provider, Medicaid paid a base rate of $1,000/month, with additional payments for someone with more challenges, like Jennifer had with her father.

After four months as a full-time caregiver, Jennifer asked the Operations Directors of the facility and the Department of Human Services to help her learn how to make caring for her dad at home easier. She shared her frustration that even in progressive states, and where people want independence and don't want to be warehoused, it's virtually impossible for a family to take care of a loved one at home.

After some hard work challenging the system, Jennifer found several solutions. Rick's Medicaid payment was increased, and Jennifer received the authority to hire her own caregivers instead of having to take whomever the facility sent her. She also found out that she could get ten days of paid overnight respite care a year.

Besides these changes, Jennifer got truly creative and started a fund so that people could donate money on a monthly basis or give a one-time donation to support Rick's cause. While the fund didn't get a lot of activity, something always came through at the end of the month when she needed it most.

Because Rick was still young, Jennifer's biggest concern was how she would be able to continue supporting him as his disease progressed. Sooner or later, as his health declined, she would have to put him back into a full-time care facility.

Introduction

Your mother fell and broke her hip, and she is being released from the hospital but cannot go home because she needs rehabilitation and 24-hour care. Or your father-in-law has had a stroke and is paralyzed on one side and is wheelchair-bound. Or your older brother has dementia and needs around-the-clock supervision. Whatever the cause, you find yourself in the situation where your loved one can no longer live independently and needs full-time care, support and supervision.

You may reach this phase because your loved one's health, strength, and/or mental functions have deteriorated or as a result of some critical medical or psychological situation. Full-time assistance can be short term; necessary only for recovery from surgery or an accident, or it may be long term, for the rest of their life.

The diagnosis and prognosis will determine whether your loved one's situation is temporary or permanent. Knowing the duration will help in making a plan and determining how to pay for care. For example, if your mother breaks her hip, she will need to be in a facility that provides personal, rehabilitation, and medical services for several weeks, but at the end of that time she can go home with some part-time assistance. But if your brother has dementia, he will likely need 24-hour care for the rest of his life.

According to Longtermcare.org, someone who is 65 today at some point will need some type of long-term care services and support for three years, on average. Women generally need care longer (3.7 years) than men (2.2 years) and 20% will need it for longer than 5 years. Someone with Alzheimer's disease may need care for 6 to 7 years.

People fear the need for long-term, full-time care most because it means that they are no longer in control of their lives. They are dependent on others and feel that they are burdensome and can no longer contribute. Your loved one probably feels the same. Even if your situation is only temporary, such as a short stay in a nursing home to rehabilitate, it can be an emotional time for him or her. It may also be an emotional time for you.

And this is a condition that really brings home the fact that your loved one will not be with you forever. You may have a whole range of feelings including fear, sadness, anger, helplessness, and/or guilt. Just know that you are not alone—these are common feelings for someone in this situation.

In this section, we address the circumstances when your loved one needs 24-hour care. The section applies situation-specific information following the general Roadmap described in the Getting Started section. To review, the seven steps of the Roadmap are:

1. Have a conversation with your loved one to establish their wishes.

2. Conduct a care needs assessment to determine the kinds of care needed.

3. Conduct a financial assessment to determine what resources are available.

4. Conduct a document assessment and inventory.

5. Ensure that your loved one maintains wellbeing.

6. Create a plan.

7. Execute and review the plan.

To recap, when Jennifer's father Rick, just 55 years old, came to visit her in the Peace Corps, she noticed that something wasn't right. And when she got home from overseas, she discovered her father had built up four months of unpaid bills. He had lost his ability to manage finances and other responsibilities. Jennifer took her father to see a doctor and went through neuropsychological testing that determined he had early-onset Alzheimer's.

Here's how Jennifer implemented the Roadmap in caring for her father:

1. Have a conversation with your loved one to establish their wishes: *Jennifer was very close to her father and through the years they had discussed Rick's wishes to be at home but not be a burden.*

2. Conduct a care needs assessment: *Jennifer observed Rick as his illness progressed and affected his abilities to care for himself. She modified Rick's care and moved from part-time assistance to caring for him full-time.*

3. Conduct a financial assessment: *Because Rick was diagnosed at a young age with such a debilitating disease, Jennifer knew her father didn't have the financial support needed for his care. She explored all the standard options and many other creative options, such as Medicaid, becoming a certified Relative Adult Foster Home Provider, and creating a fund where anyone could contribute.*

4. Conduct a document inventory: *Jennifer became Rick's guardian and executor before the disease affected Rick's ability to make decisions. They completed the appropriate forms to allow Jennifer to make all the decisions when Rick was not able to make them on his own.*

5. Maintain loved one's wellbeing: *Jennifer kept Rick in their home with comfortable surroundings, his pets, and friends nearby.*

6. Create a plan: *Jennifer worked with many medical professionals and friends to create a plan that met Rick's needs as his disease progressed.*

7. Execute and review the plan: *Jennifer was proactive and took action as issues arose and Rick's disease progressed. She explored and researched all options and never stopped challenging the system to get what was needed.*

Step 1: Having a Conversation with Your Loved One

You may be tempted to take control of your loved one's situation and impose what you think is best for them; you might think that you are helping them by making the decisions. Don't! It is important to have open and supportive conversations to determine what is important to him or her and what they want for this phase of their life. If you have been having conversations with your loved one about the future all along, or if he recognizes that a change is needed and that he needs full-time assistance, or if her doctor has told her that she needs full-time assistance, this conversation may be fairly straightforward. However, if your loved one is adamant that they do not need help with their care, it may be a more challenging conversation. The only situation where this kind of conversation is not appropriate is when your loved one does not have the capacity to participate fully in the conversation.

If they understand the circumstances and agree that they need full-time care, your conversation will be more about supporting them and understanding their goals at this time in their life. However, if your loved one does not agree that he or she needs help, it can be a difficult conversation for both of you.

Unless there is a health or safety risk, and if time allows, we recommend that you have several conversations over a period of time. Perhaps you live out of town or you're very concerned for their safety—don't try to force it all in one visit. Don't feel you have to hurry and get it done in one conversation. You're dealing with a progression of change over time, and it's most important to understand their concerns and wishes. Unfortunately, if your loved one is adamant that they can live independently without full-time help, something serious may have to happen before they change their mind, such as a fall, unreasonable or paranoiac fear of a burglary or theft, or a fire in a pan on the stove.

Your goals for the conversations are to understand what is important to them at this phase of their life, to help them recognize the need for full-time care, and to get an agreement to plan for full-time care. The first goal of the conversations is to determine what is important in four main categories: financial, home, activities, and work. It is very helpful to know what is important so you can help your loved one live a life that is as close to their wishes as possible, even if it isn't possible to meet all their wishes in the current circumstance. Ask what fears he has and how his family can help him deal with those fears. Ask her if she feels the children are responsible for her care and how she envisions that.

Don't be afraid to talk about aging and get the "scary stuff" out from the dark corners and on the table. Face it head-on, as uncomfortable as it may be; it will allow you to look at all the possibilities and opportunities that might be waiting to be discovered. It's amazing how much more comfortable you will both be when you take away the unknown of "what if" and replace it with the "when this happens, I'll be ready" concept.

Help your loved one identify goals for how and where he or she will live: for example, remain in their current home at all costs, downsize to a smaller home, move in with family, or move to a care facility. Help identify financial goals: for example, do they want to leave money for their heirs, to have a safety fund in the event of future emergencies or crisis, or to spend whatever they have to be comfortable? What kind of social or family activities do they want to participate in: pursue a hobby, be involved in the community, and be involved with family and grandchildren?

You do not want your loved one to feel that you're taking over; they want to feel included in determining what to do. He or she may not be able to have all of the things that they want, but if you know what is important to them, you will be able to help them get closer to their wishes.

Planning the Conversations

If family members or friends will be involved, have a discussion with them to determine who will be the best person to broach the subject with your loved one. It may be you, or someone else may be better suited. For example, if the person is your mother and the two of you know how to push each other's buttons, you may not be the best person. But if she has a friend from whom she is used to getting advice, that friend may be able to have a productive conversation.

We recommend that whoever is going to have the first conversations should take time in advance to think about any concerns. Are you anxious about the conversation? How is the loved one likely to react? What examples can be shared to convey concern? Whatever the concerns, take some time to prepare strategies for a difficult conversation that may have worked for you in the past. Approach the conversation with an open mind and expect a positive outcome.

If you have the luxury of time, pick a time and place where your loved one will feel most comfortable having this conversation; make the conversation convenient and as comfortable as possible. These kinds of conversations are not typically 5-minute discussions; allow plenty of time.

Having the Conversations

Ask for permission to discuss the topic. Approach the subject honestly and directly. For example, you may open with, *I can see that you are having challenges with certain things. I would like to talk with you about how we can make things easier for you. Could we do that now?* Then give one or more examples of real things that you have observed. Or, *The doctor says you need to go to a facility; can we talk about that now?*

Be a good listener. Listen to what they have to say without interrupting, giving your opinion, or telling them what to do. Rather than offer advice, guide the conversation so they can work things out for themselves as they talk.

Pay attention to body language. Observe facial expressions, gestures, posture, and other nonverbal clues. Their words may say that they agree, but their body language says, "I hate this."

Help your loved one explore the situation by asking open-ended, non-threatening questions like, *What specifically concerns you?* or *How do you feel about that?* Periodically, repeat what you've heard them say in your own words to ensure that you have a clear understanding of their wishes and ask them to do the same to be sure they understood.

Use "what if" scenarios. He or she may have a friend or family member who recently suffered a traumatic event that required them to consider senior housing or another kind of care that he or she can relate to. *Are you aware of the different housing and care options? Which of the options appeals to you? Which do you want to try to avoid? Have you thought about how you'll pay for such housing and care?*

Don't make promises you may not be able to keep or talk in absolutes such as *never* or *always*. Making a promise like, "We'll never put you in a nursing home," or "You can always come and live with us, we'll take care of you." isn't recommended. You might be tempted to say something like that to smooth things over or to make the conversation easier. You may even feel it is true, at the time, but it can lead to bad feelings or feelings of guilt down the road if you are unable to keep your promise.

Express your support. Throughout the conversations, tell them how much you love them, how important this is, and how you want to work together to find answers to these tough questions.

Step 2: A Care Assessment— Getting the Help Needed

When we talk about continuous care for your loved one, we mean providing care and supervision 24 hours a day. Even though they need round-the-clock care, they may not need care with everything, so you will want to determine where they need help—and where they don't. He or she should be encouraged to continue to do those things that he or she is capable of doing.

"Help" refers to a number of services that provide non-medical and/or medical care for people who cannot provide the care for themselves. In general, people require three types of help:

- **Self-care**: Eating, walking, bathing, dressing, toilet, or transferring—from bed to wheelchair, for example

- **Living assistance**: Light housework, preparing meals, taking medications, shopping for groceries or clothes, using the telephone, and managing money

- **Professional healthcare**: Medical or psychological assessment, wound care, medication instruction, pain management, disease education and management, physical therapy, speech therapy, or occupational therapy

The first step is to determine the level and type of care needed. If your loved is still living independently, you can spend the time to observe what they can and cannot do. You can also ask where they think they need help. If the need for care is as a result of a health or psychological issue, his or her physician may be able to help with the assessment. A geriatric care manager (also known as elder care manager, senior healthcare manager, or professional care manager) can assist you in assessing the amount and type of care that is needed. A geriatric care manager helps individuals and families adjust and cope with the challenges of aging or disability. They can conduct a care planning assessment to identify needs, problems, and eligibility for assistance. Refer to *Choosing a Geriatric Care Manager* in the **Other Considerations** section of this book for additional information.

Step 3: A Financial Assessment— Determine What Resources Are Available

Now that you know the amount and type of care that is needed, your next step is to determine how to pay for it. It is very likely that the care that is needed is going to be very expensive. It is ideal if your loved one planned for a situation such as this and you are fully aware of their plan. If so, you are well ahead of the game. If you have not discussed finances recently, you may want to do the assessment to update your understanding of the situation.

On the other hand, you may have no idea about the state of your loved one's finances or if any plans even exist. Many times people find out that there is nothing in place. It can be especially shocking when it is your parents, the people who seemed to provide for themselves and family all of your life, or your spouse, the person who handled the finances during your marriage. If your loved one does not have a plan or you do not know the state of his or her finances, we recommend that you do an assessment together to determine the financial situation.

It may be especially challenging if your loved one is in the hospital and you do not know where the information is kept or if they refuse to discuss it with you. While you may feel like you are invading their privacy, it is important that you both have a shared understanding of the finances before a plan can be put in place. Your primary goal is to help them get quality care.

Conduct a careful financial assessment to determine and document income, assets, insurance, and debts so you both have a clear and complete financial picture.

Outside Sources

Medicare. If your loved one is 65 years or older, they probably have Medicare. It is essential to know what Medicare covers: for example, Medicare pays for inpatient hospital care for up to 90 days. Some people wrongly assume that Medicare will cover the costs of long-term care whether it is provided in the home, in an assisted living residence, or in a nursing home. It doesn't. If your loved one has been in the hospital for at least 3 days, Medicare will pay for up to 100 days (about 3 months) in a skilled nursing facility—if skilled nursing is needed—or up to 100 days of home healthcare. After 100 days, your loved one will need another financial source to cover the costs.

Medicare does pay for most visits to the doctor, preventive care, hospital outpatient and laboratory tests, x-rays, mental healthcare, and some ambulance fees. It may also provide coverage for prescription drugs. Understanding the Medicare system is no simple task. For more information on Medicare coverage go to the Medicare website at: www.medicare.gov.

Private-pay Medical Insurance. Most medical insurance, including Medicare supplemental (Medigap) insurance, does not pay for long-term care costs. To determine what is covered, you will need to refer to the policy. Make a note of the cost of the premiums for the debt and expenses assessment.

Long-Term Care Insurance. Long-term care insurance is intended to cover the cost of care at home or in a facility, for individuals whose chronic disabilities make independent living difficult. Those disabilities may be physical or they may be cognitive. Long-term care insurance does not cover medical care or short-term care such as rehabilitation following an illness or hospitalization.

If your loved one has already purchased a long-term care policy, it can defray the cost of long-term care. However, once a health crisis has occurred, purchasing long-term care insurance is no longer an option.

Veterans Administration. If your loved one is a veteran or is the spouse of a deceased veteran, he or she may be entitled to benefits. Veterans' benefits may include a pension, healthcare, and nursing home or assisted living facilities. Check with his or her local or regional Veterans Affairs office to see if they qualify. There are organizations that can help navigate the VA; some are free, others charge a fee for their services. To access the Veterans Affairs website, go to www.va.gov. To locate an organization to assist you, do an Internet search for assistance with VA benefits.

Social Security. If your loved one is over the age of 65, they may get monthly Social Security payments. Social Security helps, but it is probably not enough on its own. The Social Security Administration's website (www.ssa.gov) has information and interactive tools, and an account can be set up and benefit information viewed online.

Medicaid. For older persons who have limited income and resources, Medicaid is a needs-based program available to pay for a variety of services as determined by the state in which your loved one lives. The funds for this program are provided jointly by the federal government and by state governments. Medicaid can pay for medical costs not covered by Medicare, and unlike Medicare and other health insurance policies, Medicaid can pay for long-term care. Depending upon the state in which your loved one lives, Medicaid dollars may be used for long-term care in the home or in a facility.

In order to qualify for Medicaid, there are both income and resource limitations. Those limitations can vary from state to state, although the federal government, through the Centers for Medicare and Medicaid Services, sets limits or standards as to what your loved one can own and still be eligible for Medicaid.

For married couples, if only one person needs Medicaid, the spouse who is well and can live at home or in a facility other than a nursing home is permitted to keep enough assets to permit them to live independently.

As there is more demand for long-term care, stricter rules have been made to ensure that people do not impoverish themselves by giving their assets away for the purpose of qualifying for Medicaid. And, if those applying for Medicaid have given away their assets, they will be penalized by not being eligible to receive Medicaid benefits. When recipients of Medicaid die, the state may seek reimbursement for the benefits that they have received. Generally, anything that the Medicaid recipient owned on the date of death is potentially available for recovery by the state. For example, if the Medicaid recipient's name was left on any asset (most commonly seen on a deed) then the state may claim the Medicaid recipient's share of the asset. This doesn't refer to assets that were legitimately transferred, whether sold or given away; only to something on which the Medicaid recipient's name remains. For information on Medicaid in your loved one's state, go to www.medicaid.gov.

Own Assets

Private Home*:* If your loved one owns his or her home and has equity in it, the home may be a source of income, either through an equity loan, reverse mortgage, rental income, or sale.

- **Equity Loan**: Your loved one may be able to borrow against the equity in his or her home to provide money to pay for expenses. This is the best option *if* they plan to continue to own the home and have the ability to make the mortgage payments on the outstanding mortgage *and* the equity loan.

- **Reverse mortgages**: For someone who wants to remain living at home, a reverse mortgage on a primary residence may be an option to generate income. The name "reverse mortgage" describes what it is: the homeowner, upon qualifying for a reverse mortgage, receives payments instead of making payments.

Because there are costs—sometimes considerable—for qualifying for and obtaining a reverse mortgage, it is an option appropriate only for someone who will be able to live at home for five years or more, a common benchmark. These costs can include a loan-origination fee, appraisal fee, third-party closing costs, and a mortgage insurance premium. Borrowers who cannot pay these costs directly can finance them through the reverse mortgage.

To qualify for a reverse mortgage, homeowners must be 62 or older and remain living in the home. There are no income requirements for a reverse mortgage, but the recipient(s) must be able to continue to pay property taxes, insurance, and upkeep on the property.

If the homeowner becomes ill, is hospitalized, and later must spend time in a nursing home, absences of less than a year are permitted. However, if the homeowner is out of the home for a year or more, then the mortgage will be due and payable.

Similarly, when the homeowner dies, the reverse mortgage must be repaid. How much equity, if any, is left at that point depends upon the amount of money paid from the loan, the interest rate, and any home appreciation. Usually, the home is sold and the mortgage is paid. If the loan balance is less than the value of the house, the difference is paid to the homeowner's heirs. One important protection of reverse mortgages is that the homeowner or the heirs will never owe more than the value of the home at the time the home is sold or the loan paid. This is true even if the value of the home has declined.

Payments from a reverse mortgage can be made in a variety of forms. The homeowner can receive a lump sum, monthly payments, or establish a line of credit; some lenders provide a combination of these payment forms. The important thing to remember is that reverse mortgages should be used for their intended purpose: that is, to provide care or assistance to enable a senior to remain living at home.

There are, however, no restrictions on how funds from a reverse mortgage can be used. And, unfortunately, there have been instances where borrowers have taken money from a reverse mortgage to buy luxury items or take "a trip of a lifetime" and afterward did not have enough remaining to pay for necessities.

- **Rent or Sell**: If your loved one must move out of their home, they may be able to rent or sell the house to generate additional funds.

Additional Real Estate: If your loved one owns a vacation home or investment property, they may be able to borrow against it, get rental income, or sell the property.

Other Resources

There may be additional resources set aside, such as bank accounts, mutual funds, stocks, bonds and/or an IRA, pension fund, or other qualified plan. Do they receive income from a trust? Can those payments be increased? What about a pension or an annuity? Regardless of the resource, always stop to assess the tax consequences of any of the financial decisions you make.

Contributions From Others. Can you or family members contribute funds to your loved one's care?

Debt Assessment

Once you know the sources of income, determine all debts and projected expenses including mortgage or rent payments, insurance premiums, utilities, other loan payments, necessities, and entertainment.

Let's look at a couple of examples of how funds may be applied in different situations.

Example 1: Your 80-year-old dad breaks a hip, goes into the hospital, has surgery, stays in the hospital for three weeks, and then is moved to a skilled nursing facility for four months.

Event	Paid By
Hospitalization	Medicare—up to 90 days Medicare supplemental insurance and private pay, if needed.
Physicians, tests, X-rays, medication, and surgery	Medicare, Medicare supplemental insurance and private pay, if needed.
Skilled Nursing Facility first 100 days	Medicare
Skilled Nursing Facility after 100 days	Private pay

Example 2: Your grandmother is in a wheelchair and needs assistance with all self-care and with providing for all her needs at home. Your parents hire a home-care professional agency to provide 24-hour care for her in her home. Since she has not been hospitalized in the last 10 days, Medicare will not cover the costs. But if she meets her policy's requirements for initiating her benefits, her long-term care insurance may be available to help

with the expenses. If she does not have long-term care insurance, your grandmother will need to pay for care with private funds or Medicaid, depending on her finances and the state in which she lives.

Step 4: Document Inventory and Assessment

It is critical that you have a clear and complete picture of all the documents in place to protect your loved one as he or she ages, and to be able to locate them quickly if you need to access them without the assistance of your loved one. It is important to have the following documents in place *before* they are needed.

Documents Every Adult Should Have

- **Durable Power of Attorney for Healthcare**. Enables your loved one to appoint someone to make healthcare decisions on their behalf if they cannot make the decisions for themselves.

- **Advanced Healthcare Directive**. Combines a durable power of attorney for healthcare and a statement of healthcare wishes for end-of-life care.

- **Living will**. Allows your loved one to expresses his or her wishes for the type of healthcare they want and do not want at the end of their life.

- **Power of Attorney**. Allows your loved one to appoint someone to make financial decisions and financial transactions on their behalf. A durable power of attorney remains in effect even if your loved one loses capacity.

- **Will**. States how assets should be distributed when your loved one dies. In most states, this distribution requires court involvement.

- **Living Trust.** States how your loved one's assets will be managed during his or her lifetime, who takes over management if he or she becomes incapacitated, and how their assets are to be distributed at the time of death. Usually there is no court involvement.

If these documents are not in place and the need for them arises, you will likely need to hire an attorney and go to court to get authority to make healthcare and financial decisions. This can be both time-consuming and costly. See *Documents Every Adult Should Have* in the **Other Considerations** section of this book for information to help you determine which documents are needed.

Personal and Business Documents

The last step in planning is to make an inventory of various personal and business documents, account numbers, policy numbers, and locations, to simplify access when you or someone else needs it in the future. The list includes but is not limited to:

- Bank names and account number(s),
- Birth certificates,
- Brokerage firm names and account numbers,
- Deeds on real estate owned,
- Divorce decrees,
- Education and employment records,
- Insurance policies (including company names and policy numbers),
- Maiden name (if applicable),
- Marriage certificates,
- Medicare card and number,
- Military discharge papers,

- Mortgage documents,

- Passports,

- Pets' names and veterinarian's phone number,

- Religious affiliation and name of clergy,

- Social Security card and number,

- Spouse death certificates,

- Any other appropriate personal or business documents.

Step 5: Maintain Your Loved One's Wellbeing

Regardless of the kind of care your loved one needs, it is important that he or she maintains the highest quality of life—mental, physical, and emotional wellbeing—and as much independence as possible at this phase of life.

Wellbeing is not available by prescription, and there is no one path—it is unique to each of us. A sense of wellbeing is a state of mind that depends not only on our thoughts, feelings, and actions but also on what happens to us, the events and circumstances of our lives, and the genes and personality we were born with.

Depression and loneliness are very common in aging seniors, many times occurring when social circles change due to family and friends moving away or passing on, or when they lose their autonomy, because they have difficulty seeing, hearing, or walking. Obvious symptoms of depression are changing social patterns: they may stop going out, have difficulty sleeping, appetite loss, or a change in activities—they may stop reading or engaging in conversation.

Unfortunately some discount the symptoms and describe the situation as, "They're just getting old." Also, normal changes in the brain occur with aging; sometimes cognitive decline cannot be avoided, but in other cases, keeping the mind stimulated or interacting with others may help ward off isolation and depression. Certain illnesses such as Alzheimer's disease or other dementias can make it more difficult to learn new information or remember things.

Tips for Maintaining Wellbeing

Nurture a Social Network

Now that your loved one needs 24-hour care, he or she could become isolated. It's beneficial to maintain close personal relationships with family members, friends, members of their religious community, neighbors, and other important people in their life. Encourage those close to them to visit as often as possible. You can set up a social calendar for them to ensure that they have visitors. Plan a get-together once a month.

If there are not many people geographically close, technology like email, Skype, or Facebook can play a key role in keeping people connected. According to data from the Pew Research Center's *Internet & American Life Project,* the 74-plus demographic is the fastest-growing group across Web-based social networks. Use of sites like Facebook and Twitter among Internet users 65 and older grew 100 percent between 2009 and 2010, from 13 percent to 26 percent. Many assisted living centers have even begun offering technology classes to get seniors online and in the social-networking loop. Younger family members or friends can help your loved one to use the computer. This is a great way for grandchildren to spend time with their grandparents.

Play "Mind" Games

Regularly doing crossword puzzles and playing chess and other intellectually stimulating games keeps the mind active, and playing games with others helps them to stay socially connected to peers. Scientists believe that both your body and your mind follow the principle "use it or lose it." So think of these games as fun ways to exercise the brain.

Soothe the Soles and Hold Hands

Foot massage is a highly beneficial treatment for the elderly. A non-invasive treatment, it helps to induce relaxation, which in turn aids the body's own healing processes. It can be perfect for those who no longer get out and about, as a foot massage can be enjoyed from the comfort of a favorite armchair. Massage for other parts of the body can relieve the general aches and pains associated with getting older—and everyone deserves a little pampering, especially in their later years. Along the same line as a foot massage, a manicure can create that human connection.

Share a Snapshot of Life

Getting out the family album and reminiscing is a great way for your loved one to reconnect with what is important to them. Encourage them to take the lead in storytelling; many seniors have travelled the world and can relive their journey as if it were yesterday. Everyone has a story to tell and all of us enjoy remembering birthday celebrations and events with humorous anecdotes. It is a healthy way to spend the day, sharing laughter, joy and love with each image.

Music Is Food for the Soul

Music brings out many emotions, and being in touch with our feelings and working through them is as important at 95 as it is at 5. Indulging in a game of "Name That Tune" not only exercises the mind but also brings joy and entertainment to the day.

Share Experiences

We all have our own favorite hobbies and pastimes and sharing these is an ideal way, not only to get to know someone, but also to develop other interests. It could be stamp collecting, coin collecting, or flower pressing; regardless of the activity, it is healthy and fulfilling to develop meaningful companions who share the elderly person's interests and love of life.

Meditation

Meditation, regardless of your spirituality, yields numerous benefits for those young and old. Many older meditation participants are reaping the benefits that meditation teaches for the trials of old age.

There are many resources online or in bookstores that give instructions on how to meditate, including CDs or videos that go through a guided meditation or teach the simple steps to get started. Here are a few of the health gains associated with meditation:

- **Lowers blood pressure and relieves tension that can cause high blood pressure**. More scientifically speaking, the process of meditation influences the production of nitric oxide, which widens your blood vessels. Some physicians are suggesting meditation along with other lifestyle changes such as diet and exercise.

- **Relieves stress**. Stress is a killer that can lead to many medical complications. As we get older the chance of stress triggering health conditions such as a heart attack or asthmatic episode is ever more likely. Daily meditation reduces stress and teaches techniques to control stress in a tense situation.

- **Clear-mindedness**. One reason meditation is often associated with Eastern religion is because its clarity-induced state is essential to those spiritual pursuits. Meditation allows for peacefulness and clear thought. Since the elderly are often more concerned about mortality, this allows for spiritual reflection regardless of religious beliefs.

- **Focuses memory**. Meditation can also assist with the onset of dementias such as Alzheimer's disease. A study from the University of Pennsylvania suggests that daily meditation slows down the progression of Alzheimer's. The study shows that participants who meditated just 12 minutes a day had increased blood flow in their brains. The participants also tested for improved memories.

- **Pain management**. A study at the University School of Medicine indicates that pain discomfort was greatly reduced in test subjects who were meditating. This sort of technique, if effective, would be invaluable to those with chronic pain.

- **Sleep**. Proven to be effective with insomniacs, meditation can help with sleep patterns.

Get Out

If your loved one is able to get out of the house or care facility, take them for a ride in the car or visit favorite spots or friends/family. Depending on his or her ability, you can take him or her out for a meal or to a movie.

Step 6: Creating the Plan

Once you know your loved one's wishes, the kind of care that is needed, and the financial resources that are available, you can help them to choose the best option for housing and care.

Option 1: Stay at Home and Bring in Professional Help

If your loved one's preference is to remain in their home, you can hire professionals to come into the home to provide care.

This is generally an expensive option and therefore may not be a feasible one.

For help with self-care and living assistance (non-medical assistance), you need a home care professional. The average cost in the U.S. is approximately $20 per hour or $165,000 per year for round-the-clock coverage. This is an average cost—it can be significantly more or less expensive depending where your loved one lives. A home healthcare professional is needed for medical-related assistance. The average cost in the U.S. is approximately $30 per hour or $250,000 per year, for full-time, 24-hour care.

Option 2: Augment with Family

If family and friends could provide some of the assistance (at no cost), it would reduce the costs of professional care. For example, an adult child might move in and provide the living assistance services and self-care services at night and on the weekend. A home care professional may be hired for service, weekdays during the day, and a home healthcare professional hired to come in for a couple of hours at a time, several times a week. In this example, the cost could be reduced to as low as $50,000 per year.

Instead of a home care professional during the weekdays, an adult daycare center may be an option. Adult daycare centers are designed to provide care and companionship for seniors who need assistance or supervision during the day. The cost and payment structure varies by center and geographic location and the national median daily rate is $65. This could bring the non-medical care down to $16,500 per year.

Option 3: Moving in with Family

It might not be practical for a family member to move in to provide care, but it may be possible for the senior to move in with a family member—for example, a parent moving in with an adult child. If family members work outside the home, a home care professional may be hired for service, weekdays during the day, and a home healthcare professional hired to come in for a couple of hours at a time, several times a week. This type of combined assistance, augmented by family (at no cost) could cost an average of $50,000 per year.

An alternate option would be an adult daycare center, weekdays during the day, at a national median cost of $65 per day, which could bring the non-medical care down to $16,900 per year.

Before making this decision, carefully evaluate whether you can add another dependent to the family's home, and whether you are able to care for a loved one with complex needs and still maintain quality of life for everyone. Transitioning your loved one into your home will affect the whole family and each family member's needs should be considered in the decision. A discussion with the loved one's physician is also advised.

Option 4: Nursing Home/Skilled Nursing

A nursing home is a residence for people that require continuous care and typically has both skilled nursing and non-medical care and supervision around the clock. Services usually include skilled nursing services, rehabilitative care, medical services, self-care services, and activities. Costs for nursing homes vary by facility and geographic location. The average cost for nursing homes range from $50,000 to $200,000 per year; the median annual cost for a semi-private room is $75,555 and $83,950 for a private room.

Option 5: Moving Into an Assisted Living Facility

Assisted living facilities are suited for someone who does not need round-the-clock medical care, but does not want to or cannot live independently. Assisted living facilities come in all sizes from a residential home with only a couple of residents to larger facilities with hundreds of residential units. A resident can start out living independently in their own apartment and add more care as it is needed. Services vary by facility but they typically provide both self-care and living-assistance services such as dressing, bathing, apartment cleaning, laundry, meals, and transportation. Most do not offer full-time medical attention. The national median cost is $3,450 per month ($41,400 per year), and can be higher or lower depending on the facility and the geographic location.

Note: A continuing care retirement community (CCRC) is not an option at this point unless your loved one is already a resident in one. Most CCRCs require that the resident be totally independent at the time they join the facility. A CCRC provides a continuum of care including independent living, assisted living, and nursing home care, usually in one location, and usually for the individual's lifetime.

Following is a comparison of the national median rates for services and facilities, according to the *Genworth Cost of Care Survey 2013*.

Service	National Median Rate
Homemaker Services (Licensed): Provides "hands-off" care such as helping with cooking and running errands. Often referred to as "Personal Care Assistants" or "Companions."	$18/hour*
Home Health Aide Services (Licensed): Provides "hands-on" personal care, but not medical care, in the home, with activities such as bathing, dressing, and transferring.	$19/hour*
Adult Day Health Care: Provides social and other related support services in a community-based, protective setting during any part of a day, but less than 24-hour care.	$65/day
Assisted Living Facility (One Bedroom—Single Occupancy): Provides "hands-on" personal care as well as medical care for those who are not able to live by themselves, but do not require constant care provided by a nursing home.	$3,450/month
Nursing Home (Semi-Private Room): Provides skilled nursing care 24 hours a day.	$207/day
Nursing Home (Private Room): Provides skilled nursing care 24 hours a day.	$230/day

* This is the rate charged by a non-Medicare certified, licensed agency.

Refer to the **Other Considerations** section for tips on selecting a home care professional, an assisted living facility, or a nursing home.

Depending on the care plan and living arrangements for your loved one, we offer additional considerations and advice:

Home Modifications and Retrofitting

If your loved one is going to remain in their home, move to a smaller home, or move in with family members, you'll want to make the home as safe as possible. Every year millions of seniors are injured in their home from falls and burns. Therefore, the home may need to be modified or retrofitted for safety and mobility, which may cost money, but the expense will be far less costly than moving to a facility.

Modifications may include: removing throw rugs or securing them with double-sided tape, installing railings on both sides of all staircases, installing grab bars in showers and tubs, and installing drawers or sliding shelves in cabinets. In addition, changing out door handles to lever-style, cabinet and drawer pulls for C- or D-shaped handles and adding illuminated rocker-style light switches. Install lights in closets and benches near the front and back doors. Examples of retrofitting are: installation of ramps, walk-in showers, and lifts on stairs.

If you need assistance with assessing and making changes, ask your loved one's physician to refer an occupational therapist who can conduct an assessment and make recommendations.

Tips for Living with Family Members

Whether an adult child is living with a parent or a parent is living with an adult child, communication is the key to success. Discuss potential issues up front so that you both have the same expectations and to minimize misunderstandings and conflicts. Review your plans periodically to see if modifications need to be made.

Build a Support Team

You do not have to do everything yourself; build a team to help and support you and your loved one. Refer to "Building a Support Team" in the **Other Considerations** section for more information.

Documenting the Action Plan

All action plans will be different, yet at the same time, all contain the same kinds of information: the task or activity, the date and time it will take place, the name of the person responsible, and any notes. Here is an example of a simple action plan:

Task/Activity	Date/Time	Point Person	Notes
Take dad to attorney to set up and execute documents	Monday at 10:00	Don	Dad has a will and needs other documents
Contact doctor for referral to Occupational Therapist	Monday at 9:30	Phyllis	Assess to make dad's home more safe
Go through dad's desk to complete the financial assessment	Saturday at 11:00	Don	Remind dad that he agreed to do this
Research home healthcare professionals	Saturday at 9:00	Phyllis	
Dinner with family at dad's	Sunday at 5:30	Sally (Don's wife) and Phyllis	Sally to remind dad on Sunday morning

Step 7: Executing and Reviewing the Plan

Now that you have a plan, implement it, and monitor how it is going. If you need to make adjustments, update the plan and make the adjustments. Think of it as your GPS: when something changes you need to "recalculate" and adjust the plan accordingly.

Your Action Plan—A Checklist

Now that you have carefully read this section and followed the 7-Step Roadmap, here is a summary of actions that you may use as a checklist to make sure you haven't missed anything.

1. Have a conversation with your loved one to determine their wants and needs.

    a. Finances

    b. Home

    c. Activities

2. Do a care assessment to determine where they need help.

    a. Self-Care: bathing, dressing, toilet, transferring, eating, walking.

    b. Living Assistance: light housework, preparing meals, taking medications, shopping for groceries or clothes, using the telephone, managing money.

    c. Professional Healthcare: medical or psychological assessment, wound care, medical instruction, pain management, disease education and management, physical therapy, speech therapy, occupational therapy.

3. Do a financial assessment to determine how to pay for the care needed.

    a. What outside sources do they currently have?

     i. Insurance: Medicare, private pay insurance, long-term care insurance, Veteran's Administration, Medicaid.

    ii. Assets: house, investments, rental property.

    iii. Monthly income and debts: Social Security, pension, mortgage, insurance premiums.

    iv. Contributions from others: support from family members.

4. Determine what documents are in place and where they are located.

    a. Durable Power of Attorney

    b. Advanced Healthcare Directive

    c. Living Will

    d. Power of Attorney

    e. Will

    f. Living Trust

    g. Social Security number and card

    h. Military card/Service papers

    i. Insurance Policies

    j. Legal Documents

    k. Tax Returns

5. Ensure your loved ones' wellbeing.

    a. Nurture their social network.

    b. Create activities to exercise their mind and body.

    c. Hold hands, massage feet.

    d. Create family albums, look at family pictures and read to them.

    e. Play music.

    f. Try meditation.

g. Take them out if possible; see a movie, go to a park, visit friends.

6. Create the plan with your loved one using all the information you've collected.

    a. Some options:

        i. Stay at home and bring in professional help

        ii. Augment with family members

        iii. Nursing Home/skilled nursing

        iv. Assisted Living

        v. Continuing care retirement community

        vi. Home modifications and retrofitting

        vii. Create a budget

7. Execute and review the plan often.

WHEN A CRISIS HITS

Crises refine life. In them you discover what you are.

—Allen K. Chalmers

Tom and Mary: Their Story

An aneurysm and a burst blood vessel in her brain caused Mary to have a stroke, and she went into a coma for a month. At the time the prognosis was that she had a 5% chance of living and if she did survive, she would be a vegetable.

Mary was divorced and her son and only child, Tom, lived with her and went to college full-time. Until this crisis, Mary had been fully independent. She worked full time, traveled, and lived life fully.

Suddenly Tom was in charge—and he didn't even know how to write checks or balance a checkbook, though he was a signer on Mary's checking account. He had a part-time job to pay for gas money but otherwise was completely dependent on his mother's income for survival. Other than the checking account, Tom was not a signatory on any of his mother's accounts and didn't know anything about Mary's finances except for the funds she had in her checking account.

Mary did not have an Advanced Directive for Healthcare, and she and Tom had never discussed what she would have wanted for end-of-life care. So when it came to his mother's medical condition, Tom had to rely on whatever the doctors advised should be done.

Because Mary's boss terminated her employment after the stroke, there was no more income coming into the household. Luckily Mary's insurance continued to pay the majority of her hospital bills even after she lost her job. An attorney helped Tom set up an emergency conservatorship to give him immediate access to Mary's funds during the crisis.

Mary had not put a plan in place for a crisis; she had not executed any documents to give someone else the authority to make healthcare and/or financial decisions in an emergency. While not immediately necessary, she did have a will, but Tom was not the executor. The will had been written while Tom was a minor and Mary had not updated it after Tom turned 18.

Tom visited Mary in the hospital every day and spent the majority of the day with Mary. He called Mary's friends and family regularly to keep them up-to-date on Mary's condition. He also kept a journal of what happened each day, who came to visit, who sent flowers, and what was happening with friends so that Mary would know what she had missed.

A month later, Mary came out of the coma and was completely paralyzed on her right side, couldn't speak, and initially had no memory. She was moved to a nursing home and given intensive speech and physical therapy, which helped her regain movement, speech, and long-term memory.

Mary stayed in the nursing home for four months and when she returned home, Tom had to get full-time live-in care for her for four more months.

Tom went back to court to obtain full conservatorship over Mary's estate and had to use his mother's savings to pay for her care.

Introduction

Your mother falls, breaks a hip, and is rushed to the hospital. Your father-in-law has a heart attack and needs bypass surgery. Or, as in Tom's case, your mother has a stroke and spends the next 30 days in a coma.

When something dramatic happens, usually centering on a health issue (physical or mental) that needs immediate attention—that is a crisis! Some other examples of common crises are: a fall with a head trauma, a car accident, or dramatic confusion.

A crisis will generally have one of three resolutions:

1. The crisis is addressed and things go back to normal.

2. The crisis is addressed but now the person needs some level of ongoing assistance and care.

3. The crisis cannot be resolved and the person does not survive.

The crisis phase is typically short, but extremely intense. The highest priority is to get your loved one to safety and get their situation stabilized. You will have experts involved who will provide diagnosis, a course of treatment, and prognosis. During a crisis, decisions need to be made rapidly and there is very little time—or no time—to research and investigate options. You do not have the luxury of deliberating over decisions.

Because time is of the essence, we recommend that you only make decisions about immediate issues, and you do not make irrevocable decisions during times of uncertainty. Once the outcome is known, longer-term decisions and those requiring irrevocable actions can be made.

The primary role of family during a crisis is to be your loved one's advocate. Clearly they cannot chase down the doctor in the hospital or run out to the nurses' station to get attention, get online and look up answers, express their wishes, or find other doctors for second opinions—but you can.

A crisis is also extremely emotionally charged for everyone. Your loved one will probably experience fear of what is happening to them and what it means for the future. That fear may trigger feelings of anger, frustration, and/or helplessness. You may feel those same emotions, but you might also feel resentment and guilt: resentment that their crisis is impacting your life, guilt over your frustration and resentment, or even guilt that you were not able to stop it from happening. On the other hand, you may feel hope or determination. You may have movement back and forth between all of these emotions. Do your best to get control of your own emotions before making any critical decisions.

In this section, we will provide situation-specific recommendations following the general Roadmap described in this book's introduction for actions you can take during and after the crisis to provide for your loved one's need for support, and respect for his or her independence. How you will carry out these actions depends on whether or not your loved one is capable of making and communicating decisions. To review, the seven steps of the Roadmap are:

1. Have a conversation with your loved one to establish their wishes.

2. Conduct a care needs assessment to determine the kinds of care needed.

3. Conduct a financial assessment to determine what resources are available.

4. Conduct a document assessment and inventory.

5. Ensure that your loved one's wellbeing is maintained.

6. Create a plan.

7. Execute and review the plan.

Mary did not have a plan in place, and here is how that failure to plan impacted Tom's ability to implement the Roadmap:

1. Have a conversation with your loved one to establish their wishes: *The stroke put Mary in a coma, which eliminated any opportunity for Tom to have a conversation with his mother. They never talked about her wishes before the crisis, because they never anticipated that Mary would have a stroke at age 59.*

2. Conduct a needs assessment to determine the kinds of care needed: *Once the stroke happened, Mary was hospitalized for over a month, where the doctors and medical staff made the decisions for her care. Although Tom did not have a Power of Attorney for Healthcare, he was considered Mary's surrogate.*

3. Conduct a financial assessment to determine what resources are available: *Tom had no idea what financial resources his mother had except for what was in her checking account. Because he had no access to Mary's finances to pay for living expenses and hospital expenses, Tom had to hire an attorney and set up an emergency conservatorship to give him immediate access during the crisis.*

4. Conduct a document inventory: *Mary had not executed any documents that would give Tom the power to take care of her healthcare needs or her finances and she had not updated her will as Tom's age changed.*

5. Ensure that wellbeing is maintained: *As Mary's only child, Tom took full care of his mother and helped her stay connected with her family and friends. He did whatever he could to keep her comfortable and maintain as much independence as possible in her condition. Tom ensured that his mother got the attention she needed from the medical staff of the hospital and nursing home.*

6. Create a plan: *Tom didn't formally create a plan but put things in place as Mary's condition changed; he simply handled the things that came up the best he could. He got a temporary conservatorship immediately, and a full conservatorship later when it was determined that it would be quite some time before Mary could handle her own affairs again. Tom didn't make any irrevocable decisions and made sure Mary was always taken care of.*

7. Execute and review the plan: *After a month, Mary was out of the woods and moved to a nursing home; Tom then modified her care and support based on her new condition and abilities at the time.*

Step 1: Having a Conversation with Your Loved One

Your ability to carry out this step during a crisis depends greatly on whether or not your loved one is conscious and capable of making and communicating decisions. If they are unconscious or unable to converse, move on to the next step in the Roadmap. However, if they are conscious and capable of having discussions, begin here.

Conversations during a crisis may be the hardest of all because there may not be much time and everyone is likely to be emotional. The two most important outcomes of the conversation are to ensure that your loved one understands what has happened and what they want—and do not want—to happen. Unlike the scenarios described in other sections of this book, you may have limited time and may get to have only one quick conversation with them. It is still extremely important to have the conversation and to involve him or her as much as possible. The person conducting the conversation is important too; if possible, choose someone to whom your loved one will be most receptive and listen.

You may first have to describe what has happened and where they are. You might think that this is the doctor's job, but the doctor is not always available to describe the situation. Your loved one may be at home and the Emergency Medical Technicians (EMTs) have gone or they may be in the hospital in the Intensive Care Unit (ICU) and the doctor has moved on to someone else's crisis. Start by asking them if they know where they are and why, and what is happening.

If they do not know what has happened, where they are, or have the facts incorrect, fill in the blanks for them. *"You fell. You broke your hip. You were rushed to the hospital."*

If there is going to be follow-up treatment, be sure they understand what is involved. Again, the doctor may have told you or another family member the next steps, but may not be available to discuss it with the patient. *"The doctor wants you to have surgery today to set your hip."*

If there is a prognosis, you want to make sure that they understand it as well. *"After the surgery, they will send you to a nursing home for rehabilitation. After that you can go home, with some help."*

If there are decisions to be made, help your loved one weigh the options and make a decision. If there is only one course of action, help them accept that course of action.

Your loved one may have questions that you cannot answer; let them know that you will get the answers for them. We recommend writing the questions down so you won't forget and add any questions that you have.

You'll also want to discuss how they are feeling; don't be afraid of what they might say. It will help to know what they fear, for instance, and you may be able to dispel the fear. You can also share what you are feeling. Understand your—and your loved one's—emotional reactions before you make any decisions, because strong emotions may make it impossible for either of you to think clearly.

Keep having conversations throughout the entire process to keep them up-to-date on status and next steps. Don't assume that they remember what was said in previous conversations.

Step 2: A Care Assessment— Getting the Care Needed

Follow the remaining steps of the Roadmap whether or not your loved one is conscious and able to communicate. If they can communicate, involve them in each step.

The doctors in charge, as well as other members of the healthcare team, are your key sources of information. Find out what the doctor knows about the condition: the diagnosis and prognosis, what tests (if any) are needed, recommendations for treatment, and what decisions need to be made. This information will help you determine the next steps.

Now is the time to get your questions and your loved one's questions answered. Refer back to the list you made during the conversation with your loved one and take notes as the doctor talks so that you can refer to them later as needed.

If you have the time, you may want to bring in another doctor for a second opinion on the diagnosis and course of action. You may also have the opportunity to get online and research the condition and treatment to learn more about what the doctor has said.

If your loved one cannot make healthcare decisions for him or herself, because they are incapable for any reason, someone will need to make those decisions on their behalf. If a Durable Power of Attorney for Healthcare, an Advanced Healthcare Directive, or Living Will has been executed documenting their wishes and an agent has been appointed to make healthcare decisions on their behalf, involve the designee as soon as possible.

If your loved one has not executed documents describing their wishes or appointed someone to make healthcare decisions on their behalf—and time is of the essence—someone may be able to act as a surrogate. A surrogate can speak for the loved one for a specific episode and can make decisions for a finite period of time. Healthcare-decision surrogacy laws are state-specific. Search the Internet to find laws for the state in which your loved one lives to see if the state allows for a surrogate to step in, who can be made a surrogate, what level of authority is allowed, and for how long. Refer to *Step 4: Document Assessment* for more information on these documents.

If your loved one needs someone to make decisions for a longer period of time than is allowed for surrogates or the state does not allow for surrogates, you may need to contact an attorney to get a conservator or guardian for your loved one.

Step 3: A Financial Assessment— Determine What Resources Are Available

Whatever the course of care necessary, there will be costs associated with it. If your loved one is in the hospital, you will have to provide insurance information, including Medicare and private pay insurance. Ideally, you or another family member has this information already; if not, you may have to go to their home and go through their files to find the information.

The priority is to handle your loved one's finances appropriately during the crisis. Depending on the length of the crisis, there may not be any need to deal with any finances until the crisis is over. If your loved one has executed a Power of Attorney appointing someone to handle their finances—and that person is not you—you will need to contact the agent and copies of the Power of Attorney will be needed. However, if there is no Power of Attorney and the amounts are small, you (or someone else) may be able to make the payments from personal funds. If the costs are too high or the crisis is longer term, a conservator or guardian for the estate must be appointed by the court. Refer to *Step 4: Document Assessment* for more information on these documents.

Once the crisis has passed, you and your loved one can conduct a careful financial assessment to determine and document income, assets, insurance, and debts so you both have a clear and complete financial picture based on the post-crisis situation.

Step 4: Document Inventory and Assessment

In Steps 2 and 3, we mentioned certain documents that your loved one should have in place. It is critical that you have a clear and complete picture of all the documents in place to protect your loved one as he or she ages, and to be able to locate them quickly if you need to access them without the assistance of your loved one. It is important to have the following documents in place *before* they are needed.

If your loved one does not have these in place, and they are capable of executing documents, they may want to execute these immediately. We especially advise you to do so if surgery is recommended, due to the possibility of complications.

Documents That Every Adult Should Have

- **Durable Power of Attorney for Healthcare**. Enables your loved one to appoint someone to make healthcare decisions on their behalf if they cannot make the decisions for themselves.

- **Advanced Healthcare Directive**. Combines a durable power of attorney for healthcare and a statement of healthcare wishes for end-of-life care.

- **Living will**. Allows your loved one to express his or her wishes for the type of healthcare they want and do not want at the end of their life.

- **Power of Attorney.** Allows your loved one to appoint someone to make financial decisions and financial transactions on their behalf. A durable power of attorney remains in effect even if your loved one loses capacity.
- **Will.** States how assets should be distributed when your loved one dies. In most states, this distribution requires court involvement.
- **Living Trust.** States how your loved one's assets will be managed during his or her lifetime, who takes over management if he or she becomes incapacitated, and how their assets are to be distributed at the time of death. Usually there is no court involvement.

If these documents are not in place and your loved one cannot make decisions for him or herself for a longer period of time, you will likely need to hire an attorney and go to court to be able to make healthcare and financial decisions. This can be both time-consuming and costly.

State-specific laws determine whether or not you will need a guardian or a conservator for your loved one. The conservator or guardian is appointed by the court. A guardianship or conservancy removes someone's right to make decisions for themselves and gives the legal right to another person who then becomes responsible for the food, care, housing, and financial and medical decisions for someone who is determined to be either partially or fully incapable of providing for themselves.

We also recommend that you work with an Elder Law Attorney or an attorney who is well versed in conservatorship or guardianship law. Since you are removing someone's civil rights, it is very important that you work with experts who understand what documents are needed, timelines, state laws, and many other details to support you in this action. To find an Elder Law Attorney in your loved one's area you can access a national directory on the website for the National Academy of Elder Law Attorneys (www.naela.org).

Once the crisis has passed, you and your loved one can do a more in-depth assessment of the documents that they have. See *Documents Every Adult Should Have* in the **Other Considerations** section of this book for information to help you determine which documents are needed.

Step 5: Maintain Your Loved One's Wellbeing

Even though you are in the middle of a crisis, you want to ensure that your loved one experiences the highest quality of life for the situation. If you are able, spend time with them and let them know they are loved. It is a frightening time and neither of you should be alone; you'll both feel better being together.

As an advocate, you will need to ensure that he or she gets the attention they need from the medical staff of the hospital and are as comfortable as they can be.

Help them pass the time—only a few hours can feel like days during a difficult time. If they are conscious and capable of reading, bring them magazines or a book by their favorite author. Bring in movies that they can watch on a laptop or tablet if they cannot or do not want to read. Or download their favorite music on an MP3 player and give them headphones so they can listen without disturbing others.

Contact family and friends and let them know the situation. Encourage them to visit if it is appropriate.

Step 6: Creating the Plan

Now that you have all of the information, you are ready to create a custom plan for your loved one. Make a list of all the tasks that need to be handled. Prioritize the tasks and assign due dates/times. If you have the help of others, delegate and determine who will handle each task.

If there are additional items that need to be put into place, add them to the plan. For example, if your loved one will need to go to a nursing home or assisted living facility after being discharged from the hospital, start researching facilities now.

All action plans will be different; at the same time, all contain the same kinds of information: the task or activity, the date and time it will take place, the name of the person responsible, and any notes. Here is an example of a simple action plan:

Task/Activity	Date/Time	Point Person	Notes
Talk to mom to ensure understanding of situation	Today	Tiffany	Write down list of mom's questions
Family meeting to make a list of questions	Today	Dillon	Combine with mom's list from Tiffany
Set up meeting with medical team	Today	Tiffany	
Get insurance information	Today	Dad	
Research documents in mom's state and get forms	Today	Tiffany	
Help mom execute documents	Today	Dad and Tiffany	
Research nursing home in area	Tomorrow	Dillon and Dad	Talk to hospital discharge dept. first

Step 7: Executing and Reviewing the Plan

Now that you have a plan, implement it, and monitor how it is going. If you need to make adjustments, update the plan and make the adjustments. Think of it as your GPS: when something changes you need to "recalculate" and adjust the plan accordingly.

Once the crisis is over, if your loved one needs part-time or full-time assistance, read the appropriate section of this book to get further assistance and create a plan for that situation.

Your Action Plan—A Checklist

Now that you have carefully read this section and followed the 7-Step Roadmap, here is a summary of actions that you may use as a checklist to make sure you haven't missed anything.

1. Get your emotions under control as best you can.

2. Have one or more conversations with your loved one.

   a. Confirm their understanding of the situation.

   b. Determine what they want—and don't want—to happen.

   c. Gain an understanding of their feelings and concerns.

3. Determine their current condition, diagnosis, and recommended treatment.

4. Obtain insurance and financial information to ensure treatment is conducted.

5. Determine if your loved one has their legal documents in order or, if possible, execute any that they may need.

6. Ensure your loved one's wellbeing by advocating for him or her to ensure that they get the attention they need.

7. Create a plan for the current situation and for the period after the crisis is over.

PREPARING FOR WHAT MIGHT HAPPEN

Failure to prepare is preparing to fail.

—John Wooden

Introduction

The earlier sections of this book help you deal with situations where your loved one needs some level of assistance. Those sections were reactive in nature.

This section, on the other hand, is proactive planning for what *might* happen; it will help you prepare for the future. Being proactive and taking certain steps now before they are needed will prevent a huge amount of stress later.

And you will see that the format is different from the other sections because the information outlined can be used by anyone who wants to ensure they have a plan in place before a crisis happens. It's written as a general roadmap with steps for anyone to use. Use it yourself or help a parent or loved one set up his or her own plan.

At the end of this section under **Helping Loved Ones Create their Plans,** we've included a section called "Having Conversations with Your Loved One." It will help you broach the subject with your loved one. The conversation with him or her will ensure their wellbeing is kept at the forefront when you work with them to design their plan. Then just follow steps one through six in this section.

In reality, as you are caring for your parents or loved ones, you begin to look at your own life and ask, "What am I doing to prepare for old age?" How will you make sure you get the care you need? And most important of all, how will you protect your children and other loved ones from the experiences you've had to go through in caring for your parents or loved ones? Planning for how we wish to be cared for when we are old and having the financial support we'll need is just like planning for retirement.

It's frightening to think about becoming incapacitated or needing assistance, and these are difficult topics to talk about too. We believe that planning ahead for these situations is one of the kindest things an aging adult can do for themselves and for those who will support them as they age. Defining what you do and don't want takes the guesswork out of decisions down the road, and it can help to maintain good relationships between family members and friends. Nothing can tear a family apart like disagreements about care of an ill or aged loved one and disposition of assets.

In this section, we will follow a slightly modified version of the general *Seven Step Roadmap* described in this book's introduction to address the actions you can take to plan for your health and wellbeing as you age.

Step 1: Determine Your Wishes

Your first step is to determine what is most important to you in these four categories: finances, home, activities, and work. From this you can determine what has been done and what still needs to be done, if anything remains.

- **Finances:** Do you want to be as financially independent as possible; have a safety fund in the event of emergency or crisis; buy a second home; or leave an inheritance?

- **Home:** How do you want to live? Do you want to remain in your own home for as long as possible; live close to family; relocate to another city; downsize to a smaller home; or move to a retirement or care facility?

- **Activities:** What kind of activities do you want to be involved with so long as you remain healthy and active? Do you want to pursue a hobby or take classes; be involved in the community or do volunteer/charity work; travel; or be involved with your family and grandchildren?

- **Work:** If you are still working, what are your wishes? Do you want to work as long as possible or retire soon; or do you want to start a new business?

As you work through this process ask yourself:

- *What is most important to me?*

- *What specifically concerns me?*

- *How do I feel about that?*

- *What if I couldn't get up and down the stairs anymore?*

- *What if I couldn't drive anymore?*

- *What if I suddenly needed help with certain activities of daily living?*

- *What would my wishes be if I could no longer live at home without assistance?*

Once you know your wishes, you can move through the remaining steps of the Roadmap and create a plan.

Step 2: Determine the Kind of Care You Want

Now is the time to carefully think through your wishes for your healthcare and physical care as you age, plan for long-term care, and document your health situation—current and past. Articulate what it is you do and don't want in the event you become incapacitated and cannot make decisions for yourself.

Healthcare Decisions

The first step is to make sure that your healthcare wishes are followed in the event that you cannot make decisions for yourself. This involves detailing the type of care that you want—and do not want—and appointing someone to carry out those wishes if you are unable to make your own healthcare decisions.

The person you appoint is called an "agent." The agent must be 18 years of age or older and have the ability to carry out your wishes. Your agent may be a family member, friend, spouse, or partner, and should not be a healthcare provider or an employee of a healthcare provider. You can also appoint a back-up or secondary agent. (Be sure to check your state's laws for specifics.)

Next consider the type of care you want—and do not want. Consider the type of care you should receive, by whom, and where care is given, including the use, removal or refusal of artificial nutrition, hydration, or any other decision to prolong life. Include your wishes with regard to pain management, medications, and life support, and under what conditions they should be given or withheld. For example

- Do you want to be put on life support under all circumstances or only if it is expected to help?

- Do you want to be kept pain-free even it means that you'll sleep all of the time?

- Do you want whatever medication/treatment your doctor recommends or prescribes or do you want alternative medications/treatments explored?

Once you have selected an agent(s) and determined the type of care you want, you should discuss your wishes with your agent(s) to be sure he/she/they understand fully and is/are willing to take on this role.

To put this plan into place, you must complete certain legal forms. See *Step 4: Essential Documents and Necessary Forms* for the forms to complete to document your decisions.

Long-Term Care Planning

Long-term care is the assistance or supervision you may need with the activities of daily living (ADL). The requirement for assistance could be the result of a stroke, illness, or injury, or from issues related to advanced age. You will need to determine how you will pay for long-term care if it is needed at some point in your life.

An estimated 70% of people over the age of 65 will need long-term care in some form, lasting up to three years, during their lifetimes. According to the *National Clearinghouse for Long-Term Care Information*, the average cost for long-term care in the United States in 2010 was: $75,000 per year for a semi-private room in a nursing home; $84,000 per year for a private room in a nursing home; $40,000 per year for a one-bedroom unit in an assisted living facility; and $21 per hour for a home health aide. Please note that these amounts are averages; actual costs could be significantly more in the area where you live.

Because it is likely that you may need long-term care at some point and that paying for it can be very costly (and only likely to get more so), it is important to put a plan in place. There are generally four ways to pay for long-term care.

- First is *Medicare*, which only pays for long-term care under very specific situations and then no longer than 100 days. Unfortunately, most people incorrectly think that Medicare will pay for long-term care once the person reaches 65.

- Second is *long-term care insurance*, which pays or reimburses for covered long-term care costs in a facility or for home care.

- Third is *personal resources*, such as your income and resources like bank accounts, stocks, or financial support from family members and friends.

- Fourth, is *state-provided Medicaid*, which pays only if the person meets the state's poverty guidelines.

Long-term care insurance is intended to cover the cost of care, such as care at home or in a facility, for individuals whose chronic disabilities make independent living difficult. Those disabilities may be physical or they may be cognitive. Long-term care insurance does not cover medical care or short-term care such as rehabilitation following an illness or hospitalization.

If you have already purchased a long-term care policy it may defray the cost of an assisted living facility for those who can afford to keep up with the premiums and who are in good health when they purchase the policy. However, you must be in a good health at the time the policy is issued; you cannot purchase long-term care insurance once a health crisis has occurred.

Step 3: A Financial Assessment— Determine What Resources Are Available

After you have your healthcare plan in place, the next step is to make sure you have a plan for managing your finances. This includes understanding your income, debts, and assets, and planning for someone to make financial decisions for you if you are unable to make them yourself.

Financial Decisions

Following the steps you took to ensure you have someone to carry out your healthcare decisions in the event you are unable, you should also appoint someone to make financial decisions and conduct transactions on your behalf in the same circumstances. Again, you will want to choose someone who is trustworthy, knows what you want, and will do what is best for you. It is important that this person be someone who is good with money and who makes good financial decisions. That person you select for your finance management may not necessarily be the same person you selected for your healthcare agent, but it can be.

To put this plan into place, you will need to execute a power of attorney (POA). Do you want the POA to go into effect as soon as the document is executed or do you want it to go into effect only if you become incapable of making your own decisions? Do you want it to be in effect if you become incapacitated or do you want it to terminate at that point? The POA and other documents are detailed in *Step 4: Essential Documents and Necessary Forms*.

Financial Inventory

At this point, you have outlined your wishes and the ways you want to be cared for. Now it is time to do a financial inventory to determine if your plan for paying for the life you want to live and the expenses you may encounter is feasible. If you have no formal plan or if the plan you do have is not practical, the inventory will help you to understand your financial situation so that a feasible plan can be put in place. It's never too late to put together a plan; however, it may be more challenging the longer you wait.

First consider how you will pay for healthcare. Healthcare is extremely expensive in the U.S. and is expected to get more expensive over time. Depending on the types of health issues you may face, you could easily have to pay upwards of $10,000 out of pocket per year, outside of what is covered by Medicare or long-term care insurance.

Next, determine how you will pay for day-to-day living expenses. And lastly, consider how you will finance the things you want to do to enjoy this phase of your life.

We will start by determining the sources of income and assets that you have, and then address debts and expenses.

Resources from Outside Sources

Medicare. Since the cost of healthcare is so expensive, and most Americans have Medicare coverage, we will start there. Medicare is governmental medical insurance and it covers most visits to the doctor, preventive care, hospital outpatient, hospital inpatient, laboratory tests, x-rays, and mental health care. It also may provide coverage for prescription drugs and some ambulance fees. Medicare, Medicare supplemental policies, or standard health insurance policies will NOT cover the costs of long-term care, whether that care is provided in the home, in an assisted living residence, or a nursing home. Medicare is somewhat complicated and if you are not familiar with how it works, it would be advisable to do some research. For more information on Medicare coverage go to the Medicare website at: www.medicare.gov.

Veterans Administration. If you are a veteran or the spouse of a deceased veteran you may be entitled to benefits. These benefits may include a pension, healthcare, and care in a nursing home or assisted living facility. Dealing with the bureaucratic red tape of filing a claim and receiving benefits can be frustrating; however, there are organizations that can help navigate the VA—some are free while others charge a fee for their services. To access the Veterans Affairs website, go to www.va.gov. To locate an organization to assist you, do an Internet search for assistance with VA benefits.

Medicaid. For older persons who have limited income and resources, Medicaid is a needs-based program available to pay for a variety of services as determined by the state in which you live. The funds for this program are provided jointly by the federal government and by state governments. Medicaid can pay for medical costs not covered by Medicare, and unlike Medicare and other health insurance policies, Medicaid can pay for long-term care. Depending upon the state in which you live, Medicaid dollars may be available for long-term care in the home or in a facility.

In order to qualify for Medicaid, there are both income and resource limitations. Those limitations can vary from state to state although the federal government, through the Centers for Medicare and Medicaid Services, sets limits or standards as to what you can own and still be eligible for Medicaid. For married couples, if only one person needs Medicaid, the spouse who is well and can live at home or in a facility other than a nursing home is permitted to keep enough assets to permit them to live independently.

As there is more demand for long-term care, stricter rules have been put in place to ensure that people do not impoverish themselves by giving their assets away for the purpose of qualifying for Medicaid. And, if those applying for Medicaid have given away their assets, they will be penalized by not being eligible to receive Medicaid benefits.

When recipients of Medicaid die, the state may seek reimbursement for the benefits that they have received. Generally, anything that the Medicaid recipient owned on the date of death is potentially available for recovery by the state. For example, if the Medicaid recipient's name was left on any asset (most commonly seen on a deed) then the state may claim the Medicaid recipient's share of the asset. This doesn't refer to assets that were legitimately transferred, whether sold or given away—only to something on which the Medicaid recipient's name remains. For information on Medicaid in your state go to www.medicaid.gov.

Private Medical Insurance. You may also have private insurance or supplemental insurance. You will need to refer to the policy to determine exactly what is covered. In addition to the insurance coverage, make note of the amount of the premiums and the frequency of payment to include in your inventory of debts and expenses.

Long-Term Care Insurance. If you have long-term care insurance, be sure to make a note of the amount of the premiums and payment frequency to include in the inventory of debts and expenses.

Social Security. Most likely you are or will be eligible to receive Social Security. Social Security helps but is probably not enough on its own. The Social Security Administration's website (www. ssa.gov) has information and interactive tools. You can set up an account and view benefit information online.

Your Own Assets

In addition to outside resources, you probably have assets you can use to pay for expenses or to generate income.

Retirement Assets. If you have planned for this time in your life, you may have resources set aside such as an IRA or other qualified plan. Consider the distribution schedule and various distribution options. And, do not forget to take into account the tax consequences of distribution. What other resources do you have? Do you have bank accounts, mutual funds, stocks and/or bonds? Do you receive income from a trust? Can those payments be increased? What about a pension or an annuity? Regardless of the resource, always stop to assess the tax consequences of any of your financial decisions. We also recommend that you consult your financial advisor, if you have one, to assist in determining the appropriate financial decisions.

Private Home. If you own your home and have equity in it, the home may be a source of income, either through an equity loan, reverse mortgage, rental income, or sale.

- **Equity Loan.** You may be able to borrow against the equity in your home to provide money to pay for expenses. This is the best option if you plan to continue to own the home and have the ability to make the mortgage payments on the outstanding mortgage *and* the equity loan.

- **Reverse mortgages.** For someone who wants to remain living at home, a reverse mortgage on a primary residence may be an option to generate income. The name "reverse mortgage" describes what it is. The homeowner, upon qualifying for a reverse mortgage, receives payments instead of making payments.

Because there are—sometimes considerable—expenses for qualifying for and obtaining a reverse mortgage, it is an option appropriate only for someone who will be able to live at home for five years or more, a common benchmark. These costs can include a loan origination fee, appraisal fee, third-party closing costs, and a mortgage insurance premium. Borrowers who cannot pay these costs directly can finance them through the reverse mortgage.

To qualify for a reverse mortgage, homeowners must be 62 or older and remain living in the home. There are no income requirements for a reverse mortgage, but the recipient(s) must be able to continue to pay property taxes, insurance and upkeep on the property.

If the homeowner becomes ill, is hospitalized, and later must spend time in a nursing home, absences of less than a year are permitted. However, if the homeowner is out of the home for a year or more, then the mortgage will be due and payable.

Similarly, when the homeowner dies, the reverse mortgage must be repaid. How much equity, if any, is left at that point depends upon the amount of money paid from the loan, the interest rate, and any home appreciation. Usually, the home is sold and the mortgage is paid. If the loan balance is less than the value of the house, the difference is paid to the heirs or beneficiaries. One important protection of reverse mortgages is that the homeowner or the heirs will never owe more than the value of the home at the time the home is sold or the loan paid. This is true even if the value of the home has declined.

Payments from a reverse mortgage can be made in a variety of forms. The homeowner can receive a lump sum, or monthly payments, or establish a line of credit; some lenders provide a combination of these payment forms. The important thing to remember is that reverse mortgages should be used for their intended purpose; that is, to provide care or assistance to enable you to remain living at home.

However, there are no restrictions on how you can use the funds from a reverse mortgage. And, unfortunately, there have been instances where borrowers have taken money from a reverse mortgage to buy luxury items or take "a trip of a lifetime" and afterward did not have enough money remaining to pay for necessities.

- **Rent or Sale**. If you plan to move into a facility you may be able to rent or sell your house to generate additional funds.

Other Real Estate. If you own a vacation home or an investment property, you may be able to borrow against it, get rental income, or sell the property.

Debts and Expenses

Now that you know your income and assets, the next items to look at are debts and expenses to determine if you have enough income to cover your needs. Include payments for the following items: mortgage/rent, car loan/lease, other loans; insurance (health, homeowners, car, long-term care, life); taxes (income and property); utilities (gas/electric, phone, cable, Internet); food (dining out, groceries); gasoline; clothing; entertainment; personal care; healthcare; pet care; gifts and miscellaneous.

Now that you have a picture of your financial strengths and gaps, you can come up with a plan to meet your needs.

Step 4: Essential Documents and Necessary Forms

Health Inventory

In the future, should a situation arise where you need immediate medical attention, the healthcare provider will probably ask (or provide a form asking) lots of questions about your current health and health history. Therefore, it is important that you and other family members have this information readily available.

We recommend that you record the following information, keep it updated, and put it in a place that other family members can access if needed. Include information on: current health conditions or anything for which you are actively being treated (e.g., diabetes, heart disease, arthritis, depression); allergies; a list of all medications you are currently taking; whether you wear glasses, contacts or hearing aids; a list of past procedures and/ or surgeries; and a family medical history—any conditions that your parents or siblings had.

Healthcare Decisions

In Step 2, you determined your wishes and the person who could act on your behalf. Now it is time to ensure that those wishes are carried out. A Durable Power of Attorney for Healthcare documents the name, phone number, and address of the agent(s) you have chosen. The type and number of forms depend on the state in which you live; each state has specific form and signing requirements (e.g., witnesses, notary, etc.).

The following people should be able to help you obtain the form: your doctor, local hospital, senior center, an Elder Law Attorney, or Caring Connections, a program of the National Hospice and Palliative Care Organization (NHPCO). You can also conduct an Internet search to find the form for your state.

To document your wishes for the type of care you would receive also depends on the state in which you live. It may be a part of the Durable Power of Attorney for Healthcare or it may require a second form called a Living Will or Advanced Healthcare Directive.

If you have already executed the proper forms, ensure that they are up to date. For instance, have you changed your mind about the type of care you want or is someone better suited to be your agent?

Financial Decisions

In Step 3, you determined who could make financial decisions for you and under what conditions. Determine whether you have executed a Power of Attorney, that it is the proper type, and that the information is up-to-date.

Note: When these forms have been executed, you should keep a copy and provide copies to your agent(s). For more information on these healthcare and finance-related documents, refer to *Documents Every Adult Should Have* in the **Other Considerations** section of this book.

Estate Planning

The next step is to document what you want to have happen to your property and assets when you die. This can be done with a will and/or a living trust. Following is information about wills and living trusts, so you can make an informed decision.

Wills

Do you have a will, is it up to date, and is the beneficiary still valid? A will is a legal document that spells out how your assets will be distributed when you die. It also spells out who will manage your assets, pay your debts and expenses, and make sure that your assets go to the right people or charities. If you have minor children, it will also spell out who will be responsible for them until they reach the age of 18. Everyone should have a will of their own; a couple should not have a "joint" will. Refer to the information *Documents Every Adult Should Have* in the **Other Considerations** section of this book for more information on wills.

Living Trust

Do you have a trust and is it up to date? You may also choose to have a living trust in addition to a will. A living trust is a legal document that partially substitutes for a will. With a living trust most of your assets (home, bank accounts, and stocks, for example) are put into a trust that is administered during your lifetime and then transferred to your beneficiaries when you die. The courts are not involved in the transfer of assets from the living trust, which could save significant time and money.

A living trust has a trustee, who is usually the person setting up the trust. You can also select a successor trustee who will step in and administer the trust if you become incapacitated and cannot manage it or when you die.

If you determine that you would like to have a living trust, the document should be prepared by a lawyer qualified to prepare estate-planning documents. Avoid non-lawyers who may call themselves a "trust specialist" or "certified planner" because they may not have had any legal training and may only be trying to sell insurance or annuity products.

Any and all of these documents can be prepared by an attorney. Refer to the **Other Considerations** section of this book for information on selecting an eldercare attorney.

Funeral Arrangements

We recommend that you put the arrangements you would like for your funeral into writing. Sometimes this is put into the will, but often the will is not opened and read until after the funeral.

Knowing what you want will make it easier to meet those wishes and it removes the guesswork at a time when it is hard for your family to make decisions. Check if your state requires a particular document to authorize postmortem decisions.

Document Inventory

The last step is to make an inventory of various personal and business documents, account numbers, policy numbers, and locations, to simplify access when you or someone else may need it in the future. The list includes but is not limited to:

- Bank names and account numbers
- Birth certificates
- Brokerage firm names and account numbers, maiden name (if applicable)
- Education and employment records
- Insurance policies (including company names and account numbers)
- Marriage certificates
- Medicare card and number
- Military discharge papers
- Mortgage documents, deeds on real estate owned
- Passports
- Pets' names and veterinarian's phone number
- Religious affiliation and name of clergy
- Social Security card and number
- Spouse death certificates
- Any other appropriate personal or business documents.

Step 5: Your Wellbeing

During Step 1, you defined your wishes for the future—the activities you want to enjoy and how you want to spend your time. In this step you will make a plan to ensure that you get to do the things that make life worth living.

As people age, they may start to feel that they no longer add any value or have purpose. This can be especially true after retirement. For many people, work is their purpose and passion. It may also be a main source of social interaction. It is important that you continue to feel that you matter, live a life filled with passion, and maintain social contacts. All three of these add to the quality of life and may even add to the length of your life. If you can no longer pursue the activities that bring you a sense of purpose and passion, what else could you do to incorporate that into your life? You may volunteer your time teaching, coaching, or mentoring others in the activity, for example.

It is also important that you maintain good social relationships with family and friends. There are so many more opportunities for social connection now than at any other point in time. The Internet and social media have greatly expanded how we communicate and interact with others. Seniors on Facebook (www.facebook.com) is one of the fastest-growing segments. It is a great way of seeing what is going on in friends' and family members' lives. You don't have to post status updates—just reading others' updates provides a sense of connection. If you want to stay current and in touch with business segments and colleagues you can use LinkedIn (www.linkedin.com). Skype (www.skype.com), a free online call and video service, is a great way to communicate with others who are not close by. You can talk to your grandkids and watch them grow. There are also Meetup groups (www.meetup.com), an online resource for groups of all kinds and interests all over the country. Joining a local Meetup group is a great way to make new friends while participating in an activity or hobby you enjoy. Of course technology is always changing; these may no longer be the popular sites, but plan to use the new equivalents.

There are the tried-and-true methods as well. Play golf with friends, go for hikes, and meet for lunch, dinner, or drinks. Just get together to visit and catch up. Travel with tour groups. Join the local senior center. If you are apprehensive about joining a group, arrange to have someone go with you the first time so you have a "wing man" (or woman).

Whatever it is that you would enjoy, make sure that you do it!

Step 6: Create Your Plan

Up until now you have just been discussing, researching, and documenting. Now it is time to pull all of the information together to make a plan. What needs to get done?

Health

Do you need to get into or stay in physical shape? Maybe you want to join a gym and/or start an exercise routine? Do you need to get a health situation under control? Maybe you need to quit smoking or go on a diet?

Do you want to get long-term insurance or get a Medicare supplemental policy? Or do you want help researching lower-cost options for the insurance you already have?

If you are considering moving into a facility at some point, set a time to research what's available and plan to visit some in the area to determine which ones might a good fit—and which ones are not. You can start uncluttering your current home now, so it is not such a big project and emotional drain at the time you decide to move.

Financial

Are there any benefits to which you are entitled that you are not receiving? Can you reduce any expenses by changing insurance plans or switching providers? Should you get a financial planner if you don't already have one to help you make the most of the assets that you do have?

Documents

Are there documents that you need to execute or do you need to update the ones you have?

Wellbeing

What are you going to do to maintain a high quality of life?

Step 7: Execute and Review Your Plan

Lastly, having a plan is all good and well, but it has to be executed. And your plan should also be reviewed periodically to make sure it is still viable.

According to the Social Security Administration, one in four people will live to be over 90 and one in ten to over 95. A plan prepared and put into place now may not be the same plan needed ten years from now. Review it and update it as often as necessary.

Your Action Plan—A Checklist

Now it is your turn to follow the Roadmap and create a unique plan for your situation.

Follow These Steps:

1. Plan and think through your wishes. Determine who will carry out your wishes if you should be unable to make healthcare decisions for yourself.

2. Make a plan for long-term care. Document important health and medical information. Bring other family members and friends into the discussions so that everybody understands your wishes.

3. Determine how you want to have financial decisions handled if you can no longer make them yourself. Conduct a financial inventory to determine your assets, income, debts, and expenses.

4. Execute any necessary documents that you do not currently have in place. Update any existing documents with current information. Record your key information and determine the location of your documents in case information needs to be accessed quickly later on.

5. Make a plan to incorporate the things into your life that you enjoy and in which you are interested.

6. Put together a plan that you can follow. Review it periodically and update as needed.

Special Section: Helping Loved Ones Create Their Plan

When helping your loved ones create their plans, it's critical that you take the time to think through how you will broach the subject with them. The information below will help you as you begin partnering with them to create their plan.

Having Conversations with Your Loved One

The first step is to have a conversation with your loved one to gain an understanding of their wishes for the future and what they may already have in place to ensure their wishes are fulfilled. This will help you determine what has been done and what still needs to be done, if anything.

Broaching the subject may be something that neither of you really wants to do. For that reason, of the four situational conversations covered in this book, this one may be met with the greatest resistance. The good news is that so long as your loved one is doing fine, you have the luxury to have these conversations over time. It does not have to be done in a single conversation; however, it is still important to plan for the conversations and not jump into them without thought.

Your primary goal for these conversations should be to determine what is important in four main categories: finances, home, activities, and work. For example: for their finances, do they want to be as financially independent as possible, to have a safety fund in the event of emergency or crisis, to buy a second home, or to leave an inheritance? With regard to their home, how do they want to live: to remain in their own home for as long as possible, to live close to family, to relocate to another city, to downsize to a smaller home, or to move to a care facility or retirement home? What kind of activities do they want and enjoy: to remain healthy and active, to pursue a hobby or take classes, to be involved in the community or do volunteer/charity work, to travel, or to be involved with family and grandchildren? If they are still working, what are their wishes: do they want to work as long as possible or retire soon, or do they want to start a new business? Once you know their wishes, you can move through the remaining steps of the Roadmap and help them create a plan.

Planning for the Conversations

First to consider is who is the best person to have the initial discussion? It might be you, or it might be someone else. For example, if your loved one is a parent who never listens to you, but always listens to your spouse, your spouse may be better suited. On the other hand, if your loved often looks to you for advice, you might be the best person for the job. Discuss your concerns with other family members and/or friends to get agreement and to decide who should have the conversation.

The first conversations should be one-on-one. Even though you might discuss it with other family members, this is not the time to stage a family (or group) intervention. Because there is no urgent need, these first conversations can be more informal. If appropriate, other family members can be brought in later when actual planning is taking place.

Next, consider your purpose for having the conversation so that you can clearly articulate it to your loved one. The last thing you want is for your loved one to misunderstand why you are bringing up planning. If they think you are trying to make plans to "put them away" or "steal their money," they might shut down. Your purpose may be to understand what they want for the rest of their life so that you can help them get it; to make sure they maintain control of their finances and healthcare; to help them make the most of the financial resources that they have; and to ensure that you and your siblings (or other family members) know what they want so you can all work together as a team and minimize disagreements.

Approach the conversation with an open mind; don't have preconceived ideas about where the conversation will go or the outcome. If you approach the conversation expecting that it will end in a fight, it probably will.

Plan when you will have the first and follow-up conversations. Pick a time and place that is convenient and comfortable for your loved one. For example, if your mom will talk more freely when your dad is not around, consider taking her out to lunch. If the reverse is true, take your dad out for a round of golf or go out for a walk.

Having the Conversations

You can casually start by sharing that you are working on planning for your future (which we hope you are doing) and would like to know what they want and have done or any suggestions that they may have.

You can also start by stating your purpose for wanting to have the conversation. They probably want the best for you, and if they understand that planning can help both of you they may be more open to it.

Once you start the conversation, listen to what your loved one is saying without interrupting, giving your opinion, or telling him or her what to do. To be sure that you have a clear understanding of what they have said, periodically repeat back to them in your own words what you've heard your loved one say to you. To be sure that they understood you, periodically ask them to summarize what they heard you say.

Pay just as much attention to what's not being said as to what is being said—observe their facial expressions, gestures, posture, and other nonverbal clues.

Rather than offer advice, let them work things out for themselves as they talk. Help them explore their situation by asking open-ended, non-threatening questions like, *What is most important to you? What specifically concerns you?* Or *how do you feel about that?*

Bring up "what if" scenarios. You can ask things like, *What if you couldn't get up and down the stairs anymore? What if you couldn't drive anymore? What if you suddenly needed help with certain activities of daily living? What would your wishes be if you could no longer live at home without assistance?* You can refer to what other family members or friends have done to use it as a conversation starter. Your loved one may have very strong opinions about someone else's situation and either agree or not with their choices.

Be honest and direct. Do not cover up or avoid talking about what they think of as negative information. Don't make promises you might not be able to keep like, *We'll never put you in a nursing home.* Or *you can always come and live with us; we'll take care of you.* Circumstances change over time and what may seem like the best solution now may not be the best solution years from now. Unfulfilled promises can only result in extreme guilt, anxiety, and pain. Instead, let your loved one know that you will keep his or her wishes in mind and do your best to help fulfill them providing it can be done safely.

Throughout the conversations, tell them how much you love them, how important this is, and how you're willing to work together with them to find answers to these tough questions. It's a progression of change over time; so most importantly, understand what their wishes are so you can assess available options to address the situation.

After the initial conversations, you can bring other family members together for planning discussions. It is very important for all family members to know what your loved one wants and that they understand the plans. Your loved one might want to meet with each family member separately, which is fine. What you want to avoid is your loved one promising an item or money to one person without the others knowing. Later on that could become a bone of contention. While your loved one might want to avoid arguments or be more comfortable with some family members than others, this could lead to problems down the road.

The ice has been broken, and you have had several conversations about your loved one's wishes. Don't stop there. Keep the conversations and discussions going as you work through the remaining six steps of the Roadmap.

Now it is your turn to follow the steps with your loved one and create a unique plan for their situation.

Follow These Steps:

1. Plan and have conversations with your loved one(s) to learn about their wishes. Bring other family members and friends into the discussions so that everybody has the same understanding. Lead follow-up discussions throughout the Roadmap steps.

2. Do a healthcare assessment. Determine your loved one's wishes should they be unable to make healthcare decisions for themselves and decide who will carry out their wishes. Make a plan for long-term care. Document important health and medical information.

3. Do a financial assessment. Determine how your loved one wants to have their financial decisions handled should they be unable to make them on their own. Conduct a financial inventory to determine the assets, income, debts, and expenses.

4. Conduct a document inventory. Execute any documents that your loved one does not have. Update any existing documents with current information. Record key information and determine the locations where documents are kept so that information can be accessed quickly later on.

5. Maintain your loved one's wellbeing; help him or her be excited about their life.

6. Create a plan. Put together a plan that your loved one understands and can follow. Execute and review the plan, and update it as needed.

OTHER CONSIDERATIONS

Gratitude unlocks the fullness of life. It turns what we have into enough, and more. It turns denial into acceptance, chaos to order, confusion to clarity. It can turn a meal into a feast, a house into a home, a stranger into a friend. Gratitude makes sense of our past, brings peace for today, and creates a vision for tomorrow.

—Melody Beattie

In this section you will find additional information on several topics that are discussed in each of the other sections of this book, including:

- Building your support team
- Important documents
- Choosing an attorney that specializes in the needs of seniors
- Choosing a geriatric care manager
- Tips for selecting a retirement facility/community.

Instead of repeating the detailed information in each section, the information is provided here. And in this section we cover two additional topics. First, how to talk to your loved one when it is time to stop driving. The last topic is for you—the caregiver—and provides tips for taking care of yourself as you take care of your loved one.

Building a Support Team

More than one person or an entire support team, which could be any combination of family members, friends, and/or fee-based service providers, may provide assistance when it is needed. Ideally, there is a central person who oversees the execution of the support plan and the coordination of the support team, and that person may be your loved one or another person. Whenever possible, involve the person who is being assisted as much as is feasible, including in the decision to bring in outside assistance, the selection of the person(s), the monitoring process, and the ongoing communication.

It is important to establish clear expectations and guidelines up front. The more detailed the guidelines, the less chance of misunderstanding and issues down the road. Everyone on the team should be aware of the overall plan at a high level. The gardener does not need to know about dispensing medication, but should know whom to call with any concerns or in the case of an emergency. The following tips are for the central person in setting up the support plan and schedule.

Determine Expectations

Before seeking someone to provide assistance, take some time to determine the expectations for this person. Taking the extra time up-front will make the process and relationship successful; it is helpful to consider questions like the following:

- What days of the week and hours do you need the person to provide assistance? What tasks do you want the person to complete?

- How often and when do you want them to complete the tasks? Are there things that need to be done in a specific way or is it up to the person to determine the best method? How do you define quality of work?

- Are there certain qualities you expect the person to have, such as honesty and/or confidentiality?

- If there are other people providing assistance, how will this person interact with the others?

- How do you want to receive communication when issues arise?

- How much lead time do you want before the person takes time off?

- If you will pay someone for the services they provide, how much, how often, and by what method will they be paid?

- Depending on the extent of the services being provided, should you have a written agreement?

Meet Face-to-Face

If you are not well acquainted with the person providing support, meet face-to-face with him or her early on (if you can) so you can get to know each other and establish your working relationship.

Clearly Define Expectations

When assistance is first being provided, clearly communicate your expectations for the person providing services. It is also important to ask the person to tell you what they expect from you. You should expect to end the first meeting with a shared understanding of his or her responsibilities.

Establish Monitoring Criteria

Discuss with the service provider the ways you will measure whether he or she is meeting the responsibilities you have established regarding work quality, adherence to schedules, adherence to specifications, your loved one's level of satisfaction, and the provider's conduct (time management, collaboration, etc.).

Reporting/Shared Communication

Maintain a central journal that records the details of the plan, medical visits, medications, finances, etc., so everyone involved has access to necessary information.

Tips for Communicating

Ongoing and open communication among the team members is essential.

Establish two-way communication ground rules. Conduct ongoing and frequent formal and informal communications to monitor the tasks and level of assistance being provided.

Consider holding "team" meetings periodically if there are multiple people providing assistance, so that everyone has the same understanding of the status and future direction. You can set recurring weekly meetings to discuss status and any changes; define the day of week, start time, length of each meeting and, if meeting by phone, who will initiate the call. It is also important to determine how you will communicate between weekly meetings if needed: what, how, when.

Determine if and how you will use various communication methods. Following is a list of communication options and the best use of each:

- Telephone: Weekly meetings, sensitive issues, urgent issues, formal discussions.

- Email: Progress report updates; non-urgent questions.

- Text Message: Urgent questions, real-time information sharing.

- In Person: Initial meeting; semi-annual/annual check ins/team meetings.

- Video Conference (e.g. Skype): Weekly meetings, sensitive issues, urgent issues, formal discussions when one or more team member is remote.

Prepare for each meeting beforehand, to make the most of the time you have. You can start by reviewing notes from previous meetings, addressing any questions that have come up since the last meeting, and raising any issues that need to be discussed. Maximize your meeting time. Be on time for any meetings. Eliminate distractions so that everyone can give their undivided attention to the meeting. Build in time for casual conversation to help build the relationship. Ask questions about—and pay attention to clues about—other team members' morale. Take and keep notes on the conversation.

Provide feedback—positive and constructive—to the person(s) providing services, whether the support is being provided by a family member, a friend, or is pay-for-service. Encourage the person to continue doing things that you think are done well and change things that you think can be done differently. It is a best practice to give the feedback as close as possible to the event.

Expand your perspective by gathering feedback from your loved one and anyone else with whom he or she interacts (e.g., other team members, doctors and medical staff, and friends and family members), and include that in your feedback comments.

Tips for Managing Cultural Differences

You may find that one or more members of the support team have cultural differences from your loved one and other team members. Here are things to consider and tips for successfully managing differences:

- **English is a second language**. Communication may be further challenged if English is not the person's first language. Speak slowly and clearly. Avoid using sarcasm or slang, which may be misinterpreted.

- **Time off.** Be aware of any religious or national holidays during which they may be unavailable to provide support.

- **Culture.** Understand the culture's norms and views on work-life balance, authority, etiquette, and modify your expectations accordingly.

Documents Every Adult Should Have

In the event you or your loved one becomes incapacitated, there are several key documents that every adult should have to ensure that wishes regarding healthcare and finances are handled by a trusted and capable person selected to do so. For all documents, we recommend that you or your loved one work with an attorney that has experience in this area, for example, an Elder Law Attorney. Because these documents require the signatory to have the mental capacity to execute these documents, they should be in place before they are needed.

Durable Power of Attorney for Healthcare

This document enables your loved one to appoint someone (an Agent) to make healthcare decisions on their behalf if they cannot make the decisions for themselves or are unable to communicate their wishes, up to and including terminating care and life support. The document will state the Agent's name, phone and address, and the Agent will have the right to make healthcare decisions for your loved one.

Laws that govern Durable Power of Attorney for Healthcare vary by state as to the form and the signing requirements (e.g., witness, notary, etc.). It is important to use the form specific to the state in which your loved one lives. The form can be found online by searching "Durable Power of Attorney for Healthcare" for the state in which your loved one lives.

The agent may be a family member, friend, spouse, or partner, must be 18 years of age or older, and have the ability and willingness to carry out your loved one's wishes. Your loved one can also appoint a back-up or secondary agent.

This is a decision that should be considered very carefully. The person appointed as a healthcare agent should be someone who will take the time to understand their loved one's wishes— what is important to them—and be prepared to follow those wishes, not their own. The agent will need to be able to act as an advocate, and be assertive and persistent. He or she may need to stand up to doctors, hospital staff, family members, lawyers, etc. without being intimidated. For example, if the physician does not agree ethically or morally with the agent's decision, the physician can refuse the decision. The agent must then find a physician who will honor the decision. And, hospitals have their own protocols that they will follow, so the agent must insert him or herself into the process if the loved one's wishes are different from the hospital's protocols.

Living Will

A Living Will clearly states your loved one's wishes for the type of care they want—and do not want—if they are unable to communicate their wishes themselves. Instructions may include the type of care given, by whom, and where it is provided; the use, removal or refusal of artificial nutrition, hydration, tests, resuscitation, or any other decision to prolong life; and organ donation.

In most cases, this document does *not* give anyone power to make decisions on someone else's behalf. The laws that govern this document are also state-specific; only use the document that is appropriate for the state in which your loved one lives.

Relationship of Durable Power of Attorney for Healthcare and Living Will

In some states, the Durable Power of Attorney for Healthcare and the Living Will are one form, in others they are two separate forms. For example, at the time of this writing California has one form that encompasses both documents, but some states have two separate documents. Any of the following should also be able to help you obtain the correct form: your doctor, local hospital, senior center, an Elder Law Attorney, or Caring Connections, a program of the National Hospice and Palliative Care Organization (NHPCO).

Regardless of when your loved one executes the documents—months or even years in advance—they do not go into effect until such time that your loved one's doctor makes a determination that he or she does not have the ability to make his or her own decisions, either because they are unable to understand the consequences of their choices or they are unable to communicate their own wishes.

The executed documents stay in effect until death unless they are revoked or replaced with an updated set of documents. In some very rare cases, a court may invalidate the documents or revoke an agent's authority. If your loved one moves to another state, new forms that are specific to that state should be executed. Because forms from a previous state of residency may or may not be recognized in the new state, it is safest to execute new ones.

After the forms are completed, your loved one should keep the original(s) and give copies to the agent, alternate agents, family members, their doctors (to be placed in their medical records), and anyone else who is likely to be contacted in a health emergency. A laminated wallet card may be handy to carry at all times; if your loved one goes to the hospital, they (or someone else) should bring it with them.

Power of Attorney

Your loved one should appoint someone to make and transact financial decisions on their behalf if they cannot do so for themselves. To do this requires a Power of Attorney (POA). POAs can be either immediate or "springing." A springing POA is not effective immediately; it only goes into effect under circumstances that have been defined in the POA document. However, if the POA is not a springing POA, it will go into effect immediately. The person appointed will be able to handle your loved one's financial affairs as soon as the power of attorney is executed.

If the POA states that it is "durable" or if there are words to that effect, the POA will remain in place if your loved one becomes incapacitated. If the POA is not described as durable (other words may be used), it terminates if your loved one becomes incapacitated.

If your loved one wants to have a POA in place so that a designated person can make decisions only if he or she becomes incapacitated and to continue until it is revoked, your loved one will want to execute a *springing, durable* Power of Attorney and define the circumstances under which it will take effect.

Will

A will is a legal document that spells out how your loved one's assets and possessions will be distributed upon his or her death. It also spells out who will manage your loved one's assets, pay any debts and expenses, and ensures your loved one's assets go to the right people or charities. If your loved one has minor children, it will also spell out who will be responsible for them until they reach the age of 18. A will goes into effect only when your loved one dies. Everyone should have a will of their own; a couple should not have a "joint" will.

A will covers all assets that are in your loved one's own name alone. It does not cover any assets that are jointly owned (joint tenants); those will pass to the surviving joint tenant at the time of death. In community property states, a will does not cover any of the surviving spouse's half of the assets owned as community property. At the time of death, your loved one's ownership in the asset passes to his or her spouse. Assets for which a beneficiary has been named, such as life insurance policies or retirement plans, are not covered by a will. Even if all of your loved one's assets are owned in joint tenancy with their spouse, they should have a will. If their spouse dies first, then all of the property will be subject to your loved one's will.

At the time of your loved one's death, your loved one's wishes will be carried out under court supervision, called Probate. The probate process differs from state to state; in some states it is a very simple process, but in others it can be complicated, lengthy, and costly. If your loved one dies without a will, the courts will make the determination as to how the assets will be distributed according to that state's law. That may mean that your loved one's assets will go somewhere other than he or she might have wanted, probably not to friends or favorite charities.

Living Trust

A living trust is a legal document that partially substitutes for a will when certain assets (a home, bank accounts, or stocks, for example) are put into a trust that is administered during your loved one's lifetime. The assets are then transferred to the beneficiaries after his or her death. The courts are not involved in the transfer of assets in the living trust (requiring no probate), which could save significant time and money.

A living trust has a trustee, which is usually the person setting up the trust. The trustee could be your loved one or someone that they have chosen. He or she can also select a successor trustee, who would step in and administer the trust if your loved one becomes incapacitated, can no longer manage the trust, or dies.

If your loved one chooses to have a living trust, the document should be prepared by a lawyer who is qualified to prepare estate-planning documents. Avoid non-lawyers who may call themselves a "trust specialist" or "certified planner" because they may not have had any legal training and may only be trying to sell insurance or annuity products.

Choosing an Elder Law Attorney

Elder law is a distinct legal field that concentrates on the special circumstances and needs of older and disabled persons. An elder law attorney has knowledge of the senior population, myths related to competence and aging, and the physical and mental difficulties that often accompany the aging process. Because of their broad knowledge base, an elder law attorney is able to more thoroughly address the legal needs of elderly clients.

Elder law covers all aspects of planning, counseling, education, and advocacy for clients. Elder law attorneys are a resource to their clients because they understand that their clients' needs may extend beyond basic legal services. They stay informed about and connected to local networks of professionals who serve the elder population. An elder law attorney will:

1. Focus his or her practice on the legal needs of older adults.

2. Work with a variety of legal tools and techniques that specifically meet the goals and objectives of the older client.

3. Use a holistic approach to legal advice, taking into consideration the key issues facing older adults: housing, financial wellbeing, health and long-term care, and autonomy/quality of life.

4. Bring to his or her practice knowledge of the issues facing people as they age, which allows them and their staff to ignore the myths relating to aging and the competence of the elderly.

5. Take into account and empathize with the physical and mental difficulties that often accompany the aging process. Their understanding of the real-life problems of people as they age allows them to determine more easily the difference between the physical versus the mental disability of a client.

6. Remain tied into a formal or informal system of social workers, psychologists, and other eldercare professionals who may be of assistance.

According to the National Elder Law Foundation, when you look for an attorney to help with an elder law issue, you should look first at Certified Elder Law Attorneys because they have demonstrated that they understand more than your legal problems, and they can help you.

The Certified Elder Law Attorney (CELA) certification has frequently been referred to as "the gold standard" for elder law and special needs practitioners. It reflects the hard work and proof required before an attorney can proudly proclaim that he or she holds the valued designation.

Preparation for a CELA designation includes multiple steps and several different types of qualification, all of which are designed to ensure that clients receive good legal care. Before being certified, an applicant must:

1. Have practiced law for at least five years, and have focused at least half of their practice in the special needs/ elder law field for at least the last three of those years.

2. Demonstrate "substantial involvement" in special needs and elder law practice, by demonstrating a minimum

number of individual cases, spread across a number of different categories making up the "elder law" definition.

3. Study for, take, and pass a rigorous, daylong written examination. Recent pass rates have hovered around 50%—and that is of applicants who have already met the experience requirements.

4. Undergo a review by peers and colleagues, focused on the applicant's reputation for ethical and competent representation in elder law and special-needs planning matters.

There are only a few more than 400 CELAs in the country, so not every community has an attorney who has been certified. You can find an Elder Law Attorney and Certified Elder Law Attorney near your loved one by searching the following websites: National Elder Law Foundation (www.nelf.org) and National Academy of Elder Law Attorneys (www.naela.org).

Choosing a Geriatric Care Manager

If you are finding that managing the issues around helping your loved one is more than you can handle, you could hire a professional geriatric care manager.

According to the National Association of Professional Geriatric Care Managers, a Geriatric Care Manager is a health and human services specialist who acts as a guide and advocate for families caring for older adults. You can think of Geriatric Care Managers as a "coach" or "team captain."

The Geriatric Care Manager is educated and experienced in any of several fields related to care management including, but not limited to nursing, gerontology, social work, or psychology, with a specialized focus on issues related to aging and elder care. They also have extensive knowledge about the costs, quality, and availability of resources in their communities.

Geriatric Care Managers are engaged to assist in a variety of areas, such as:

- **Housing**—Helping families evaluate and select the appropriate level of housing or residential options.

- **Home Care Services**—Determining the types of services that are right for a client and assisting the family to engage and monitor those services.

- **Medical Management**—Attending doctor appointments, facilitating communication between doctor, client, and family, and if appropriate, monitoring client's adherence to medical orders and instructions.

- **Communication**—Keeping family members and professionals informed as to the wellbeing and changing needs of the client.

- **Social Activities**—Providing opportunity for the client to engage in social, recreational, or cultural activities that enrich the quality of life.

- **Legal**—Referring to or consulting with elder law attorneys; providing expert opinion for courts in determining level of care.

- **Financial**—May include reviewing or overseeing bill paying or consulting with client's accountant or designated Power of Attorney.

- **Entitlements**—Providing information on Federal and state entitlements; connecting families to local programs.

- **Safety and Security**—Monitoring the client at home, recommending technologies to add to security or safety of the client, and observing changes and potential risks of exploitation or abuse.

A care plan tailored for each individual's circumstances is prepared after a comprehensive assessment. The plan may be modified, in consultation with client and family, as circumstances change.

You can learn more and find a Geriatric Care Manager in your loved one's area on the National Association of Professional Geriatric Care Managers website (www.caremanager.org).

Selecting a Home Health Care Professional, Assisted Living Facility, or Nursing Home

This is a situation where you need to be honest with yourself and the facility's staff about your loved one's capabilities and needs so that together you can determine if the place is a good fit for him or her.

In-Home Care

If you hire a professional through an agency, the professional is most likely an employee of the agency. The agency is responsible for meeting state employment laws. If you hire a professional directly, however, they may be considered your employee and you are responsible for meeting state employment laws.

When investigating a home care agency or care professionals, follow this checklist:

- Determine the staff members' credentials.
- Determine the level of training the staff members have had.
- Determine the services that will be provided.
- Determine costs and payment options, including Medicare and Medicaid payments.
- Determine the emergency procedures in place.
- Obtain references for the agency and the specific workers that will be interacting with your loved one.

- Determine that the professional(s) assigned to assist your loved one will provide services according to his or her preferred schedule and practices. For example, if your loved one is an early riser, the professional who assists with preparing breakfast and dressing will need to start work early in the morning.

Assisted Living Facility

When choosing an assisted living facility, consider the following:

- Is the facility licensed and operating legally? If the facility's license has ever been revoked, determine the reason.
- How long has the facility been in business?
- Review the facility's inspection and financial records.
- Obtain references from the facility.
- Is the facility in a safe neighborhood?
- Is the facility located close to shopping, doctor's offices, restaurants, entertainment, family and friends?
- Is public or private transportation available and accessible?
- What is the cost? How are rate increases handled; what are the discharge policies?
- What services are included in the stated cost and which are an additional cost?
- Are there behavior restrictions regarding smoking or drinking alcohol?
- Are there rules about pets?
- What are visitor policies, visitor hours, and policies regarding overnight guests?

Physically visit the facility more than once and talk to the staff and residents. Consider these questions:

- Is it a desirable style and in good shape?
- Is it clean?
- Is it safe and secure?
- What is the staff-to-resident ratio?
- Does the facility provide a private apartment or a room and private bath?
- What meals are provided? Is the food appetizing? (Eat one or more meals in the facility.)
- Do the residents seem to have their needs met and be content?
- Do the residents interact with each other and the staff in a friendly and respectful manner?
- What social/recreational programs are offered?

Nursing Homes

When choosing a nursing home, consider the following:

- Is the facility licensed and operating legally? If the license has ever been revoked, determine the reason.
- How long has the facility been in business?
- Review the facility's inspection and financial records.
- Obtain references from the facility.
- Is the facility in a safe neighborhood?
- Is the facility conveniently located close to family and friends?
- Is transportation for doctor office visits provided?
- What is the cost? How are rate increases handled; what are the discharge policies?
- Is the facility Medicare and Medicaid certified?

Physically visit the facility more than once and talk to the staff and residents. Consider these questions:

- Is it a desirable style and in good shape?

- Is it clean? How does it smell?

- Is it safe and secure?

- What is the staff-to-resident ratio? How many nurses are on duty at each shift?

- What meals are provided? Is food appetizing? (Eat one or more meals in the facility.)

- Do the residents seem to have their needs met and be content?

- Do the residents interact with each other and the staff in a friendly and respectful manner?

- What social/recreational programs are offered?

When It Is Time to Stop Driving

The time may come for your loved one to give up driving. Depending on how important driving is to him or her, it can be one of the more difficult situations with which you deal or it may be a piece of cake.

The first step is to assess whether your loved one can still drive safely. In some cases your loved one may make that decision for themselves, but in others they may not recognize when the time comes to stop driving. Here are some signs that it might be time:

- The car has new scrapes or dents.

- There are scrapes and dents on the sides of the garage.

- They have received several traffic tickets.

- Their doctor is recommending that it's time to have a conversation with them.

The best way to assess whether or not your loved one should still be driving is to take a ride with them. Are you comfortable with his or her driving or are you constantly "false braking" by pushing your foot against the floor or telling them to look out? Watch for the following:

- Do they remember where they are going and how to get there?

- Do they respond appropriately to situations such as stopping at red lights or avoiding another car?

- Are they leaving an appropriate amount of space between the cars in front of them?

- Can they easily turn their head to back up or change lanes?

- Can they follow traffic signs correctly?

If you cannot take a ride with them, find someone who can— another family member, friend, or neighbor.

Whether it is time to hang up the keys or you want to start preparing your loved one for the day that they can no longer drive, you or someone else should have a conversation with them about driving. First discuss what driving means to them, and then show that you understand and have empathy for how they feel about not driving. Discuss their transportation needs and lastly, discuss options to driving to find a solution. During the discussion follow many of the tips for having a conversation that were covered in Step 1 of the Roadmap such as listening, body language, etc. Unless they are in danger of hurting themselves and others, this can be a series of conversations over time.

Different people can feel differently about driving. For some, cars represent independence and freedom, or a feeling of status or self-esteem, but for others a car is just a means to an end or even a burden. For this reason, understanding what it means to your loved one will give you an idea of how big a challenge the situation might be.

To understand how your loved one may feel about giving up driving, imagine how you would feel and what you would do if you did not have access to a car for an extended period of time— say two months. How would you get things done, get to work, socialize, run errands, get the kids to school, go to the doctor, etc.? How would you feel about not having a car and having to find alternate means of transportation? Would you be frustrated, feel like you are imposing on others, isolated, trapped, or angry?

Share your feelings with your loved one as a way of showing understanding. You can expect that your loved one will have negative feelings about no longer being able to drive. You may find they get angry with you for just bringing up the subject and they are adamant about driving. Those feelings are about the situation and are not directed at you.

If driving is just a means to getting things done, you only need to find suitable transportation. If driving gives your loved one a sense of independence and freedom, look for transportation options that allow them to be able to go places whenever they want, such as taxis or by keeping a copy of the bus schedule in a convenient place. They may need to start planning ahead a little more in order to meet their transportation needs. If having a car is more of a status symbol than a means of transportation, allow them to keep their car—just not have the keys to drive.

Here are some obvious options for alternative transportation: friends and family, neighbors, members of the same social group, members of the same faith group, taxis, and buses. Some not-so-obvious sources may offer transportation options, such as the local shopping mall shuttles; shuttles offered by hospitals, clinics, and doctors' offices; senior or community centers and community volunteer groups (e.g., Kiwanis or Lions clubs), or ride-share programs. We suggest doing an Internet search on "senior transportation in <city>" to find additional options in your loved one's city.

Tips for the Caregiver

The responsibility of caring for a loved one can take a physical and emotional toll on the caregiver. Most caregivers are stretched in many directions, trying to keep up with their jobs, managing a household, and caring for their aging loved ones. That is why caring for yourself is one of the most important things you can do for your loved one. When your needs are taken care of, your loved one will benefit too.

Get Proper Nutrition

Everyone knows that eating right and improving your sleep habits supports your wellbeing. Caregivers usually know what to eat but just don't have the time. One recommendation is to batch-cook, which allows you to freeze individual portions that you eat during the week. Make sure you have nutritious foods that you can grab on the run like almonds, fresh fruit, peanut butter and jelly sandwiches, raw vegetables, etc. All of these help keep blood-sugar levels on an even keel and energy levels from dropping.

Get Enough Sleep

Disrupted sleep also zaps your energy, so adopt good sleep habits. Sleep in a dark room with few distractions. Take a warm bath and/or read something light and fun before sleeping instead of watching TV or the news. Try to avoid problem-solving or emotional conversations several hours before preparing for sleep. If you're still finding it hard to sleep at night, try taking naps during the day.

Reduce Personal Stress

Stress is a normal part of life but in different circumstances, like caregiving, we can experience higher levels of stress. Some caregiving situations are more stressful than others. For example, it may be more stressful to care for someone with dementia than someone with a physical limitation. Or your relationship with the person you are caring for may be strained, making it more stressful to deal with issues that arise.

No matter the situation, it is important to take steps to reduce your stress and improve your wellbeing. First, identify the source of the stress. Some sources may be doing too much, family disagreements, inability to say no, or a feeling of inadequacy. Identify what you can and cannot control or change. Remember we can only change ourselves, not someone else. So look for the things you have control over. Am I taking on too much? Do I need to ask for help? Do I have any time for me?

Some examples of stress reducers are meditation and exercise. Just twelve minutes of daily meditation can dramatically improve the mental health of caregivers. Exercise is known to calm us and reduce blood pressure. And exercise doesn't have to be hard or long. Take the dog for a walk or spend 30 minutes at the gym. Even if it means asking a friend to take over your caregiving while you go to the gym, take time to exercise.

Other examples of stress reducers include connecting with friends, even if it's for a quick cup of coffee or a phone call in the evening. Carving out time each day for you is critical. Take some time to read a magazine or your favorite book, spend some time in the garden, or go to the movies. You might also find it helpful to join a support group, keep a journal, or seek professional help. Determine which actions best suit you in supporting stress reduction and then create weekly goals to build stress-reducing practices in your daily life.

Ask for and accept help. Many caregivers find it difficult to ask for help, feeling that they don't want to burden others or to admit that they can't handle everything alone. Here are some tips for asking others for help, taking into consideration the interests or special ability of the person you are asking for help. Maybe a friend loves cooking, so ask them to help with meal preparation. If a relative loves being out of the house, ask him or her to help with running errands or driving your loved one to appointments. Be careful to not ask the same person repeatedly for help even though it might be the easiest.

Prepare a list of things that you need help with and let the helper pick which task they want to take on. Be prepared that some people may hesitate to give you an answer or say no to your request. Don't take it personally. Ask them to think about the request and leave it open. You shouldn't let this stop you from asking them at a later date. Be specific, clear and concise: "I would like to attend my son's soccer game this Sunday. Would you stay with Mom from 1-4pm?"

You may find that friends and family members ask if they can help, but you either don't want to be a burden or can't think of ways they can help. Make a daily list of everything that you need to do. When they ask, look at your list and assign them one thing. Instead of being a burden, you may be helping them. They may want to help, and feel guilty for not helping, but not know how they can help.

Find Respite Care

It is important that you maintain your interests outside your caregiving role. To do that you might need respite care to fill in for you. Call on community services—there are many local services that can help to support your caregiving. A geriatric care manager can help organize care services for your loved one. Home health aides, homemakers, and home repair services are also available to help take on some of the responsibilities of caregiving. Civic and faith-related organizations have volunteers and staff who will help with cooking, driving or just visiting your loved one when you need it. Use the Eldercare Locator (www.eldercare.gov) by entering your loved one's zip code into a free, confidential online tool that will connect you to an agency with local eldercare services.

Slow Down

No matter the task, don't rush. This sounds obvious, but when we're tired or stressed we tend to be distracted and are more prone to accidents. If you feel yourself getting agitated or feeling like you don't have enough time, just take a deep breath and slow down your actions. You will end up getting what you wanted done in the same amount of time or less because you are focused and calm. Your loved one will pick up on your emotions, so if you're rushing they may be prone to an accident. In turn, if you are calm, that will leave them feeling safe, calm, and trusting.

Volunteer

As funny as this sounds for those who feel like they don't have enough time, it's been proven to help because you get to help in a different, gratifying way And it gets you out of your normal surroundings and relating to others outside your caregiving family and community.

Here's an additional tip from Monique Snyder's book *Before the Storm:* Give yourself credit for the smallest things you have done.

RESOURCES

Give a man a fish and you feed him for a day. Teach a man to fish and you feed him for a lifetime.

—Chinese Proverb

Here are several resources to assist you in your journey of caring for your loved one(s). All these resources were available at the time this book was published; however, we have not used or read all of these resources.

Websites

AARP
AARP is a nonprofit, nonpartisan organization, with a membership of more than 37 million, that helps people turn their goals and dreams into real possibilities, strengthens communities and fights for the issues that matter most to families such as healthcare, employment security and retirement planning.
www.aarp.org

AARP Worksearch Program
Online job search assistance including resume writing, assessment to match interests to jobs and online job search feature.
www.aarpworksearch.org

Assisted Living Federation of America (ALFA)
Founded in 1990, ALFA serves as the voice for operators of senior living communities and the seniors and families those communities serve. The website provides information and a zip code locator to support you in finding a care facility near you. *www.alfa.org*

Alliance on Aging
As a community leader and advocate, the Alliance on Aging provides relevant services and resources that address the opportunities and challenges that come with aging. *www.allianceonaging.org*

Alzheimer's Association
Nonprofit dedicated to support and research to eliminate Alzheimer's disease. The website provides information, services and links to local chapters. *www.alz.org*

A Place for Mom
The website provides a senior care locator, senior care resources and a directory of senior care advisors to make caring for a senior easier. *www.aplaceformom.com*

Care Guide
Provides information to help you find eldercare providers, housekeepers, and many more services. *www.careguide.com*

Centers for Medicare & Medicaid Services (CMS)
The CMS, a federal agency and branch of the U.S. Department of Health & Human Services, administers Medicare, Medicaid and the Children's Health Insurance Program (CHIP) program in partnership with state governments, and private health

insurance programs including Health Insurance Marketplaces, and provides information for health professionals, regional governments, and consumers.
www.cms.hhs.gov

Certified Financial Planner Board
Professional organization that sets the standards of excellence for competent and ethical personal financial planning. The website has a CFP Financial Planner locator.
www.cfp.net

The Eldercare Locator
The Eldercare Locator, a public service of the Administration on Aging, U.S. Department of Health and Human Services, is a nationwide service that connects older Americans and their caregivers with information on senior services.
www.eldercare.gov

Encore Careers (formally Civic Ventures)
Encore Careers combine personal fulfillment, social impact and continued income, enabling people to put their passion to work for the greater good.
www.encore.org

Family Caregiver Alliance (Support for caregivers)
FCA is a public voice for caregivers providing programs (Information, Education, Services, Research, and Advocacy) that support and sustain the important work of families nationwide caring for loved ones.
800-445-8106
www.caregiver.org

Hospice Education Institute (Referrals for the terminally ill)
The Institute is an independent, not-for-profit organization, serving members of the public and healthcare professionals with

information and education about the many facets of caring for the dying and the bereaved.
800-331-1620
www.hospiceworld.org

Independent Living Aids (ILA, LLC)
Online shopping site for vision, hearing, mobility and daily living aids.
800-537-2118
www.independentliving.com

Meals on Wheels Association of America
Provides meals to homebound persons.
http://www.mowaa.org/

Medic Alert Foundation
Through a paid membership, it provides medical alert products and access to an entire emergency support network.
www.medicalert.org

Medicaid
Provides state specific information on Medicaid eligibility, programs and services.
www.medicaid.gov

Medicare
Official site for Medicare providing information on benefits, coverage, premiums, healthcare providers and claims.
www.medicare.gov

National Academy of Elder Law Attorneys, Inc. (NAELA)
The National Academy of Elder Law Attorneys, Inc. (NAELA) is a professional association of attorneys who are dedicated to improving the quality of legal services provided to seniors and

people with special needs. The site provides an eldercare attorney locator/directory.
www.naela.org

National Association of Professional Geriatric Care Managers
Provides information on working with a geriatric care manager and provides a locator.
www.caremanager.org

New Lifestyles
Area guide to senior residences and care options.
877-881-7907
www.newlifestyles.com

Social Security Administration
Official site of the Social Security Administration providing answers to questions, online enrollment, and benefit information.
www.ssa.gov

USA.gov
The Seniors pages provide links to government resources for seniors on money, housing, health, consumer protection, and more.
http://www.usa.gov/Topics/Seniors.shtml

Veteran's Administration
Official site of the Veteran's Administration providing information on benefits and services.
www.va.gov

Books

Aster, Bart. *AARP Roadmap for the Rest of Your Life: Smart Choices About Money, Health, Work, Lifestyle ... and Pursuing Your Dreams.* (Maine: Thorndike Press, 2013)

Attwood, Janet, Attwood, Chris. *The Passion Test. The Effortless Path to Discovering Your Destiny.* (New York: Plume, 2008)

Barry, Patricia. *Medicare For Dummies.* (For Dummies, 2013)

Boss, Pauline. *Loving Someone Who Has Dementia: How to Find Hope while Coping with Stress and Grief.* (Jossey-Bass; 1 edition June 24, 2011)

Butler, Katy. *Knocking on Heaven's Door: The Path to a Better Death.* (New York: Scribner, 2013)

Cassidy, Thomas M. *Elder Care: What to Look For, What to Look Out For!* (New Horizon Press, 3rd Edition, May 1, 2004)

Chopra, Deepak. *Perfect Health, The Complete Mind Body Guide.* (Three Rivers Press, 2000)

Connor, Jim. *When Roles Reverse: A Guide to Parenting Your Parents.* (Charlottesville, VA: Hampton Roads Publishing Co., 2006)

Delahanty, Hugh, Ginzler, Elinor and Pipher, Mary. *Caring for Your Aging Parents: The Complete AARP Guide.* (New York: Sterling Publishing, 2005)

Farr, Evan H. *Nursing Home Survival Guide: Helping You Protect Your Loved Ones Who Need Nursing Home Care by Preserving Dignity, Quality of Life, and Financial Security.* (Quality Legal Publications, LLC; 1st edition December 5, 2012)

Gross, Jane. *A Bittersweet Season: Caring for Our Aging Parents and Ourselves.* (Knopf; Reprint edition April 26, 2011)

Hallenbeck, James L. *Palliative Care Perspectives.* (USA: Oxford University Press, 2003)

Jacobs, Barry. *The Emotional Survival Guide for Caregivers: Looking After Yourself and Your Family While Helping an Aging Parent.* (New York: Guilford Press, 2006)

Lebow, Grace, Kane, Barbara and Lebow, Irwin. *Coping with Your Difficult Older Parent: A Guide for Stressed-Out Children.* (William Morrow Paperbacks; 1 edition February 1, 1999)

Morris, Virginia. *How to Care for Aging Parents. 3rd Edition* (New York: Workman Publishing, 2004)

Peterson, Jonathan. *Social Security for Dummies.* (For Dummies, 2012)

Prosch, Tim. *The Other Talk: A Guide to Talking with Your Adult Children About the Rest of Your Life.* (McGraw-Hill, 2013)

Rath, Tom, Harter, Jim. *Well Being, The Five Essential Elements.* (Gallup Press, 2010)

Shadel, D. *Outsmarting the Scam Artists: How to Protect Yourself From the Most Clever Cons.* (Wiley, 2012)

Sheehy, Gail. *Passages in Caregiving, Turning Chaos into Confidence.* (Harper, 2011)

Sibley, Brenda Parris. *Help for the Caring: a Bibliography and Filmography for Family Caregivers of Alzheimer's Patients.* (iUniverse, December 5, 2002)

Solie, David. *How To Say It to Seniors: Closing the Communication Gap with Our Elders.* (Prentice Hall Press September 7, 2004)

Weil, Dr. Andrew. *Healthy Aging, A Lifelong Guide to Your Well-Being.* (Anchor Books, 2007)

Zukerman, Dr. Rachelle. *Eldercare For Dummies.* (For Dummies, 2003)